AMERICAN LITERATURE
SHORT STORY

The Author

Basanta Barman is an Assistant Professor of English at Umeschandra College (previously City College, Morning), Kolkata. He has presented and published several papers on literary, linguistic and social concepts. Besides academic teaching of English literature and Communicative English in undergraduate courses, he has equal enthusiasm for creative writing such as poems, stories and screenplay. He has contributed poems to several anthologies with international repute. He has compiled and edited a number of books of which mention may be made of *Communicative English*, *Guide to English LCC-1: Language, Variety and Stylistics* and *CBCS English Honours CC-1 and CC-2* for the undergraduate students of Calcutta University.

AMERICAN LITERATURE SHORT STORY

Basanta Barman

CONCEPT PUBLISHING COMPANY PVT. LTD.
NEW DELHI-110059

ISBN: 978-93-5594-620-1 (HB)
ISBN: 978-93-5594-621-8 (PB)

First Published 2023

Published and Printed by

Concept Since 1974

Concept Publishing Company Pvt. Ltd.
A/15-16, Commercial Block, Mohan Garden,
New Delhi-110059 (India)
T: +91-11-41101460
E: publishing@conceptpub.com, *W*: www.conceptpub.com

Cataloging in Publication Data–Courtesy: D.K. Agencies (P) Ltd. <docinfo@dkagencies.com>

Barman, Basanta, author.
American literature : short story / Basanta Barman.
pages cm
ISBN 9789355946201 (HB)
ISBN 9789355946218 (PB)

1. Poe, Edgar Allan, 1809-1849. Purloined letter. 2. Fitzgerald, F. Scott (Francis Scott), 1896-1940. Crack-Up. 3. Faulkner, William, 1897-1962. Dry September. 4. Short stories, American--History and criticism. I. Title.

LCC PS374.S5Z56 2023 | DDC 813.0109 23

This Book is dedicated to

My Father

Late Suresh Chandra Barman

PREFACE

American Literature, in brief, depicts the dream of American people. It gives us an opportunity to know about American society, culture and its history. This genre of literature started with the hands of Washington Irving and later it became blossomed in the hands of great writers like Jacob Ralph Abarbanell, Oscar Fay Addis, Jacob Adler, Louisa May Alcott, Herman Melville, Henry David Thoureau, Ralph Waldo Emerson, Nathaniel Hawthorne, Walt Whitman, Edgar Allan Poe, F. Scott Fitzgerald and William Faulkner.

In this book, three American short stories are included for undergraduate as well as post graduate students of Indian universities. In-depth explanation has been attempted for their easy understanding and grasping the theme of the stories. ***The Purloined Letter*** by Edgar Allan Poe, ***The Crack-Up*** by F. Scott Fitzgerald and ***Dry September*** by William Faulkner have been discussed elaborately. Word notes, annotations etc. have been incorporated along with the text of the stories so that the students can grasp them effortlessly. A number of essays have been included with each story to increase their capacity of knowledge with the help of which they will be able to deliver deliberations on any topic on these stories.

At last but not the least I would like to convey my gratitude and thanks to CONCPET PUBLISHING COMPANY (P) LTD for their continuous support and encouragement to bring out this book.

Any suggestions, from any corner, to better this book, will be highly acknowledged.

Basanta Barman

VIVEKANANDA BHAWAN
KOLKATA-48
15.10.2022

ACKNOWLEDGEMENTS

1. Edgar Allan Poe, *Collected Works of Edgar Allan Poe*, ed. Thomas Ollive Mabbott (Cambridge: Harvard University Press, 1969-1978)
2. Jaques Lacan, "*Seminar on The Purloined Letter*", translation Jeffrey Mehlman, Yale French Studies (1972)
3. Jaques Derrida, "*The Purveyor of Truth*", translation W. Domingo, J. Hulbert, M. Ron and M.R. Logan, Yale French Studies (1975)
4. Collected Stories, William Faulkner, New York (1950)
5. William Van O'Connor, *The Tangled Fire of William Faulkner*, University of Minnessota Press, (1954)
6. William Faulkner, *The Sound and the Fury*, Vintage, London (1995)
7. Cleanth Brooks, *The Yoknapatawpha Country*, New Haven, Yale University Press (1963)
8. Scott Donaldson, *The Crisis of Fitzgerald's Crack-Up, in Twentieth Century Literature*, Vol. 26, No. 2, F. Scott Fitzgerald Issue (1980)

CONTENTS

INTRODUCTION

American literature as a whole comprises the written or literary activities covered in the field of the United States and its colonies. Earlier America was a British Colony especially the eastern coast of the United States. As a result American literature bears the legacy of British Colonial masters and tradition of English literature. In spite of that, the finer spirit of American nationalism and cultural tradition caused it to be considered as a separate literary entity.

The enormous, scientific, economic, social and philosophical change of the 18th century brought about the enlightenment movement in the states and as a result, it challenged the authority of clergymen and scriptures and gave way to democratic thinking. The increase of population resulted greater diversity of opinion in religious and political fields as reflected in the literature of the time. The first novel in American Literature was published in the late 18th and early19th century. Gradually women novelists appeared in the scene in the next decade.

The fiction and poetry had a profound impact on the people. This literary genre even changed the course of many a lives.

The focus was on allegorical literatures and dark psychologies. Romances filled with philosophical speculation and adventurous voyages. Literature became a medium of examining such themes as obsession, the nature of evil and human struggle against the elemental nature. Anti-transcendental works from Henry Melville, Nathaniel Hawthorne and Edgar Allan Poe comprise the dark romanticism—a sub-genre of literature that was popular during that period. The poetry of this period also was witty, ingenious, exquisitely wrought and psychologically penetrating.

The American literature of this time has the ability to transport its readers into the world of fantasy, fiction and imagination. The readers could explore and go beyond boundaries, appreciate the beauty of nature to reach the unreachable or achieve the unachievable. The American Literature especially prose and poetry had an indelible impact on the mind of the reading people. The writers and poets wished to take their readers to a world of where they can enjoy and appreciate literature and understand the writers' point of view. They aimed to provide an enriching experience that can help them enhance various realms of life. At the same time their writings provided psychological growth to the readers as well as aesthetic enjoyment.

A Brief Overview of American Literature (From early 19th century to present day)

From the beginning of the 19th century, American literature began to attract international attention, in spite of the fact that the English critics attacked them in stern and dubious manner. An English critic complimented William Cullen Bryant's poem by saying that he could not believe that 'Thanatopsis' was written by an American poet. "Leather Stocking tales" by James Fenimore Cooper lacked sophistication but at the same time Cooper had the power of telling exciting tales. That was the beginning of the American Novel. Another writer Washington Irving composed "Sketch Box" which was a short story and, thus Irving gave impetus to the new genre of the American literature. These authors initiated romanticism in American literature.

The Romantic Movement

Mystery and death were the chief themes of the American Romantic authors like Edgar Allan Poe and Nathaniel Hawthorne. They created with dexterity a sense of supernatural in their life nature. Both Poe and Hawthorne wrote ghost stories and both were perfect stylists. To mark the readers feel the present of supernatural powers, Poe used a number of poetic devices like the repetition of the ominous sounds in his poem, "The Raven and Annobelle Lee". The *Scarlet Letter* and *The House of Seven Gables*—two novels of the Nathaniel are the study of human psychology. Hawthorne's pre-occupied thought of the Calvinist doctrine of inherited sin is revealed in his works of literature. Herman Melville, a disciple of Hawthorne, employed symbolism and allegory to signify the presence of demonic forces in the lives of human beings in his *Moby Dick* and other romantic fictions of the sea.

Transcendentalism

The New England writers imbibed the influence of puritanism. But the religious tradition was losing its ground giving vent to humanistic ideals. Ralph Waldo Emerson became the pioneer of a new idealism called transcendentalism. In his writing and lectures, Emerson emphasised on individual and cultural independence.

Emerson called for a new group of writers who would defend the rights of free human spirit against subjugation of materialism. Emerson was influenced by the romantic temper of the age and he expressed his romantic ideas through his mystic approach to nature. To him, nature was a source of intellectual and artistic inspiration. Henry David Thoreau, Emerson's friend, lived in the woods for two years when he compiled his classic creation WALDEN. Thoreau waged a verbal war against the tyranny of social conventions, commercialism and governmental restrictions.

Middle of the 19th century was the golden age of the Romantic period in American literature. The leading authors were creating there mature works and the romanticism reached climax. The novel and short stories were well read and poetry has out of fashion. But poets like H. W. Longfellow, J.G. Whittier and James Russel Lowell continued writing poetry and their works were quite popular among the readers. Walt Whitman was a modern poet in his treatment of life and poetic style. But Whitman was a romantic poet in his treatment of nature and his optimism for humanism. Like Emerson, Whitman also visioned America's future in its frontiers.

Post-War Realism

When the civil war ended in America, romanticism declined. Artists and litératteurs were disillusioned by the fellow citizens and their race for life. It was seemed that the Americans were losing the faith in human nature. The second half of the 19th century was an age of scientific realism, and rapid developments were made in both science and technology. Wealthy industrialists became eager to show their riches in several social pretensions. A new horizon of learning was opened. Thomas Cowperthwait Eakins learned a realistic technique of painting in Paris and he introduced that new technique in America. John Mcneill Whistler anticipated the modern movement towards more abstract picture. He advocated a new doctrine — art for art's sake. Regionalism also gave a new life to American literature.

Authors like Bret Starfe, Joel Chandler Harris and Mark Twain in the spirit of American literary tradition, added a refreshing sense of humour. They were realistic in depicting rural scenes and the language of the people. Mark Twain was a senior writer but at the same time he was a great humorist. He used his humour as a vehicle for penetrating social criticism.

Journalism

Many American authors began their career as journalist. Mark Twain was a journalist before he became famous as a novelist. William Dean Howells was also a journalist who satirised the injustices of America's social system in his novel *A Traveller from Alteruria*. Another newspaper correspondent, Stephen Crane wrote a masterpiece entitled *The Red Badge of Courage* in which he portrayed the fears of an ordinary soldier.

20th Century Nationalism

By the beginning of the 20th century, a new sense of nationalism evolved in the minds of the American artists. They consciously developed a national style. The authors of this century were disillusioned by social and economic injustices, war and financial depression. The dominant authors of America focused on themes that expressed their dissatisfaction with the romantic idealism of the past. A new generation of authors, after the end of the war, emerged in the field of American literature, who tried to set a new trend in American fiction. They were called Lost Generation because they lived their lives without any moral purpose and they rebelled against any traditional standard of morality and taste. They gave birth to a new cycle in American Literature which was only comparable to the literature of the 19th Century romantic period.

Racial Conflict and Social Unrest

Racial conflict was more dominant in Southern part of America and it led to social unrest. William Faulkner, Tennesse Williams and Robert Penn Wanner composed literature highlighting the history of slavery and injustices of modern capitalism. After the Civil War, the white aristocracy of the South has been degenerated. These authors portrayed the Southern Whiteman's defeat, his wounded pride and his moral guilt. A number of Faulkner's books which symbolise the fall and corruption of the entire human race, focus upon the decline of South American Society. Faulkner used the "Stream of Consciousness" technique in which there is no chronological sequence of scenes and images. Dreiser's *An American Tragedy* and Fitzgerald's '*The Great Gatsby*' are two novels concerned with lust and financial power, social prestige and sexual conquest. Obviously, the characters in these novels are destroyed in the end by their own ambitions.

Period of Great Depression

Period of great financial depression increased the feelings of dissatisfaction and disillusionment among American writers. In spite of that and under current of deep love for humanity flew in their writings. Life and struggle of poor and starving farmers became a new topic of writing for writers like John Steinbeck, John Dos Passos and James T. Farrel.

Play and Poetry

Theatrical creations flourished in this century. Eugene O'Neill was the greatest playwright of this period. His theme and technique owe to ancient Greek tragedy, but he innovated his own way to writing. *The Emperor Jones*, *The Hairy Ape*, and *Mourning Becomes Electra*—all these plays of O'Neill have dominant themes. In all his plays he used drums to symbolise primitive passion and marks to contrast the outward appearance and inner reality of his character.

20th century American poetry has gone through several experiments such as its form, language and subject matter. Poetry has been no longer limited to traditional patterns and rhyme schemes. Some poets even eliminated rhyme from poetry completely. New rhythmic effects and visual appearances have been experimented by them. The ordinary speech of common man became the language of poetry. The poets tried to give a graphic design of their surrounding in their poetry. This technique came to be known as imagery and poets like Ezra Pound, Amy Lowell and T.S. Eliot are the masters of imagist technique. However, some poets composed poetry in simple and straight forward manner. As for example, Robert Frost composed poems on rural life of New England. Carl Sandburg also enumerated Frost and he is rightly called the people's poet.

Growth and Development of American Short Story

In the second half of the 19th century, short story in America yielded to a mixed package which was more prolific and impressive. But in Europe, the period was dotted with such great names as Guy de Maupassant (1850-93), Anton Chekhov (1860-1904), Leo Tolstoy (1828-1910), R.L. Stevenson (1850-94), Rudyard Kipling (1865-1936), Ivan Turgener (1813 -83) and many more. Few American short story writers were comparable to these great masters in the realm of modern short story. Among large gallery of short stories, mention may be made as the following: 'Boule de Suif' and 'The Necklace' by Maupassant; *The Darling and Ward No. 6* by Chekhov and *Family Happiness* and *The Death of Ivan Ilyich* by Leo Tolstoy are compelling masterpieces.

On the other hand, the American short story offered a curious juxtaposition of stories that were mere tissues of cleverness with those which had substance and craft, of stories, that gloried in artifice and trickery. There were two types of short stories in American literature—the popular short story and the quality short story. These two genres are not merely exclusive of each other but a number of writers combined the two. One strand grew up with facile, journalistic and unexperimental story and the other strand was serious, meaningful and innovative story. Bret Harte (1839-1914) and Stephen Crane (1871-1900) were journalistic story writers. Like a good journalist, they wrote popular American demand for a direct, fast track story of effect and they devised smart and mechanically turned out stories that earned them instant recognition and fame. They adhered to the best selling formula for writing a story with ingredients like "People humour, movement, colour, suspense, surprise, the touch of sentimentalism, the wave of regret, and the laughter behind tears. O. Henry was the great master of this formula. He had something for every body in the market place of storytelling. He had a sense of tragedy, a sympathy for the underdog and he was incessantly interested in people and could make them tirelessly interesting. He believed in surprise ending rather than trick-ending in most of his popular stories like *The Gift of the Magi* or *The Last Leaf*.

Beside the shaping and peaking of the popular American short story, the period witnessed several innovative and path-breaking writers who were seriously committed to the art of story-telling. Ambrose Bierce was purist story writer who distinguished journalism from literature. *In the Midst East of Life*, a collection of Bierce's short story, intensely reflects the personal perception of men and things. It is magic touch of impressionism and his endeavour to compress the short story to interpret character through casual and apparently irrelevant incidents anticipate the later 20th century authors. Truly speaking, Bierce remains the major or connecting link between Poe and American short story today.

Stephan Crane introduced and integrated the features and the facts of "nationalism" and "determinism" in American short story. According to Joseph Conrad, Crane never knew how good his best work was. Crane belongs to that select group of short story writers who not only enriched but also widened the range of the genre.

Renaissance in American Short Story

In the early decades of the twentieth century Sherwood Anderson (1876-1941) broke free both from the popular, mechanical and stereotypical stories of O. Henry and Bret Harte as well as the serious writing of Ambrose Bierce and Stephen Crane. He heralded the Renaissance in 20th century American short story. He took his material from indigenous ingredients and wrote authentically about the remote and obscure Americans of a wide variety living in Ohio Valley, moving "Out of nowhere into nothing". He lent colours and significance to the otherwise colourless and insignificant people by his mid western prose rhythms with a studied styleness which kept him closer to "life" than to "art". Anderson's short stories are at the same time tough and tender, and are suffused with human persistence and heavy melancholy. Anderson's short stories like *I Want to Know Why* and *Death in the Woods* are among the finest of American short stories.

Hemingway and Faulkner

Ernest Hemingway (1898-1916) and William Faulkner (1897-1962), both were initially much under the influence of Sherwood Anderson, sheared away from the older traditions of English and American short story. Hemingway, in a manner of speaking was a man with an axe and he pruned the language, evolved the "iceberg principle" of writing, started using understatement and passed on multiple meanings largely through symbolic and ironic implications. William Faulkner also pruned the language but he did so like one who prunes a tree that blossoms anew and enormously, and lends "the highest possible degree of saturation to his work. Faulkner focused all along on the regional in his case the South America. His plots and characters evoke the decadent and traditional life cycles of the aristocracy and the poor in the cities and villages of this region as well as the inbuilt social anxieties and racial tensions of their lives.

Contemporary American Short Story

The second half of the 20th century witnessed the versatile creativity in American short story. Irving composed short stories with relaxed characterisation; Poe wrote the stories with those of pre-established effect; Hawthorne's stories were close to allegory and parable and Harte's stories were competent but looked quite machine-made. Some stories registered light seriousness like the stories of Bierce and some ushered in 'nationalism' and 'determinism' such as the stories of Crane. O. Henry's short stories were surprise ending as well as trick ending whereas Anderson's stories work genuinely and firmly rooted in the regional and local colour. Hemingway's short stories were like floating icebergs on the sea but the picture of decadence and transition of the American South were drawn by William Faulkner. Besides, there were many writers with many more variety of writing styles, notably Herman Melville, Mark Twain, Henry James, Eudora Welty, Katherine Anne Porter, Richard Wright, Willian Saroyan, Bernand Melamud and many others. All these short story writers contributed stories which reflect several aspects of American life, culture and the nation at large. The second half of the 20th century also witnessed a number of new trends and developments in the field of creative writing. Changes in society brought about a change in their view towards the life also. The growth of nuclear family entrenched with high individualism, development in technology and consumerism, shifting scenes of political scenario from cold war, Vietnam war and emergence of America as the superpower, emergence of black and feminist voices, the increasing pressure of post-modern sensibility, American people begin to adjust with all these changes 'norms' and 'sense of reality'.

Authors like Robert Coover (1932), Donald Barthelme (1933) Joyce Carol Oates (1938) and John Updike (1932) have written short stories in the second half of the 20th century. Some of them have felt compelled to reexamine and redefine the concept of a short story again. And doing so, these writers came dangerously close to causing a complete collapse of artistic control in their writing. The outmoded, depleted and nearly exhausted connections of narrative paved the way for the present-day post-modern short stories which reject all norms lock, stock and farnel and leans too heavily on the tropes of parody and pastiche, of interrogation and scepticism and on the strategies of deconstruction of all imagine and artistic constructs. The post-modern story throws the entire heritage of short story upside and hence it may be called anti-story of which definitive evaluations are still in the making.

1

The Purloined Letter

Edgar Allan Poe (1809-1849)

Edgar Allan Poe was born at Boston in Massachusetts on 19th January, 1809. His parents were well known cine-couples Elizabeth Arnold Hopkins Poe and David Poe Junior. But unfortunately Edgar became an orphan at the age of only two and he was brought up in the house of Mr. John Allan, a successful Scottish merchant in Richmond, Viriginia. The Allan family gave the name Edgar Allan Poe.

Poe attended a grammar school in Irvine, Scotland and a boarding school in Chelsea, London for a brief spell of time. Then he returned to Virginia in 1820. In 1826 Poe was admitted to the one-year-old University of Virginia to study ancient and modern languages. There he became addicted to gambling and went over debts. Poe gave up study, left the university, went to Virginia and found it not a welcome place for him. So he travelled to Boston in 1827 and took several jobs from a clerk to a newspaper writer. He also tried to be enlisted in the army and by this time he started writing seriously. In 1827 he brought out his first book of poetry *Tamerlane* and other poems which was a forty-page collection of poetry and unfortunately it received no attention by the readers. Poe joined the army, spent two years' posting to South Carolina, failed to be an Officer's Cadet at the West Point, composed satirical poems about commanding officers and left the army after a deliberate court-martial. In 1831, Poe left for New York where he released his third collection of poetry. In this year, Poe felt an urge in writing prose. Success started to come. *The Baltimore Saturday Visitor* awarded Poe a prize in October, 1833 for his short story "*Mr. S. Found In a Bottle*" which caught the attention of the literary circle in Baltimore including John P. Kennedy who introduced Poe to Thomas P. White, the editor of the *Southern Literary Messenger* in Richmond. Thus, a failure poet started his new journey as a successful short story writer. During the thirties and forties Poe published a good number of short stories including *The Black Cat, The Pit and The Pendulum, The Premature Burial, The Tell Tale Heart, Ligeria, William Wilson and The Fall of the House of Usher*. In 1945, Poe again turned to his first love, the poem, and published *The Raven* which was a great success and overnight he became a household name.

Edgar Allan Poe's literary legacy is a formidable one. He is considered one of the greatest composer of Gothic and detective fiction that even lived, and popular literary culture is replete with references to him.

An Introduction to the Story

The Purloined Letter is a detective short story by the American writer Edgar Allan Poe. It is the third of his three detective mystery stories which featured C. August Dupin, the famous Parisian amateur detective. The two other stories of this genre are The Murder in The Rue Morgue and The Mystery of Marie Roget. The story was first published in December 1844 by Carey and Hart, Philadelphia, with the tittle *The Gift: A Christmas and New Year's Present for 1845*. Later it was included in the *Tales by Edgar Allan Poe*, a collection of short stories published in 1845.

The story begins with the unnamed narrator and the private detective C. Auguste Dupin, both being engaged in a discussion regarding their experience to solve the mystery in the case of *The Murder in the Rue Morgue*. The conversation of the duo interrupted by the Parisian police officer, Mr. G- who cut in their conversation and told about a certain letter that was stolen. The letter was very personal and it belonged to a woman of royal position. In the course of circumstances, the letter was openly stolen by the cunning minister D - who wants to avail of some undue political advantage with that letter keeping in his own custody. The case given to the Paris police to bring back the letter and it was Mr. G-'s responsibility to save the face of the royal, honourable woman as well as the police department. He investigated in an possible method but in were vain. So he visited C. Auguste Dupin, who was a clever private detective, with the hope that he would be able to find out a solution for him.

Later the story progresses in a linear way enabling Mr. Dupin to retrieve the valuable epistle and thus secured in his possession the prize amounting fifty thousand Francs. Later Dupin explained to the narrator how cunningly he visited the cunning minister D, surveyed his room and noticed the important letter suspending on a rack beneath the mantle-piece, left his snuff-box for the alibi that he could visit the Minister D— the next day. So he visited the minister again the next day, foxed him with his pre-planned scheme and bade him good-bye along with the snuff-box as well as the letter. Thus, Poe set a trend in this story by giving explanation of solution of mystery which is called "play fair" in the detective stories. This trend pared the way for "observation and deduction" by Sherlock Holmes and others in the world of detective literature. With this trend alone, Edgar Allan Poe stands as a stalwart and is rightly called the "Father of detective stories".

The Purloined Letter

Edgar Allan Poe

Nil sapientiac odiosine acumine nimio.
Seneca

At Paris, just after the dark one gusty evening in the autumn of 18—, I was enjoying the twofold luxury of meditation and a meer schaum, in company with my friends C. Auguste Dupin in his letter back library, or book closet, au torisieme, No.33, Rue Dunot, Faubourg St Germain, 3.4. For one hour at least we had maintained profound silence; while each to any casual observer, might have seemed intently and exclusively occupied with curling eddies of smoke that oppressed the atmosphere of the chamber. For myself however, I was mentally discussing certain topics which had formed matter for a conversation between us at an earlier period of the evening; I mean the affair of the Rue Morgue, and the mystery attending the murder of Marie Roget. I looked upon it, therefore, as something of the coincidence, when the door of our apartment was thrown open and admitted old acquaintance, Monsieur G—, the Prefect of the Parisian police.

We gave him a hearty welcome; for there was nearly half as much of the entertaining as of the contemptible about the man, and we had not seen him for several year. We had been sitting in the dark, and Dupin now arose for the purpose of lighting a lamp, but sat down again, without doing so, upon G.'s saying that he had called to consult us, or rather to ask the opinion of my friend, about some official business which had occasioned a great deal of trouble.

'If it is any point requiring reflection,' observed Dupin, as he forbore to enkindle in wick, 'we shall exam it to better purpose in the dark.'

"That is the another of your odd notions,' said the Prefect, who had a fashion of calling every thing 'odd' that was beyond his comprehension, thus lived amid an absolute lesson of 'oddities?

'Very true,' said Dupin, as he supplied his visitor with a pipe, and rolled towards him a comfortable chair.

'And what is the difficulty now? I asked. 'Nothing more in the assassination, way, I hope?'

'Oh no; nothing of that nature. The fact is, the business is very simple indeed, and I make no doubt that we can manage it sufficiently well ourselves; but then I thought Dupin would like to hear the detail of it. because it is so exclusively odd.'

'Simple and Odd,' said Dupin.

'Why, yes; and not exactly that, either. The fact is, we have all been a good deal puzzled because the affair is so simple, and yet baffles us altogether.'

'Perhaps it is the very simplicity of the thing which puts you at fault,' said my friend.

'What nonsense you do talk!' replied the Prefect, laughing heartily.

'Perhaps the mystery is a little to plain,' said Dupin.

'Oh, good heavens! who ever heard of such an idea?

'A little too self-evident.'

'Ha ! ha ! ha ! — ha !] a ha ! — ha ! ha ! ha ! — roared our visitor, profoundly amuseu, 'oh, Dupin, you will be the death of me yet!'

'And what, after all, is the matter on hand?' I asked.

'Why, I will tell you,' replied the Prefect, as he gave a long, steady, and contemplative puff, and settled himself in his chair. 'I will tell you in a few words; but, before I begin, let me caution you that this is an affair demanding the greatest secrecy, and that I should most probably lose the position and I now hold, were it known that I confided it to any one.'

'Proceed,' said I.

'Or not,' said Dupin.

'Well, then; I have received personal information, from a very high quarter, that a certain document of the last importance, has been purloined from the royal apartments. The individual who purloined it is known; this beyond a doubt; he was seen to take it. It is known, also, that it still remains in his possession.'

'How is this known?' asked Dupin.

'It is clearly inferred,' replied the Prefect, 'from the nature of the document, and from the non-appearance of certain results which would at once arise from its passing out of the robber's possession; — that is to say, from his employing it as he must design in the end to employ it.'

'Be a little more explicit,' I said.

Well, I may venture so far as to say that the paper gives its holder a certain power in certain quarter where such power is immensely valuable,' The Prefect was fond of the cant of diplomacy.

'Still I do not quite understand.' said Dupin

No? Well; the disclosure of the document to a third person, who shall be nameless, would bring in question the honor of the personage of most exalted station; and this fact give the holder of the document an ascendancy over the illustrious personage whose honour and peace are so jeopardized.'

But this ascendancy,' I interposed, 'would depend upon the robber's knowledge of the loser's knowledge of the robber. Who would dare-'

'The thief,' said G., 'is the Minister D—, who dares all things, those unbecoming as well as those becoming a man. The method of the theft was not less ingenious than bold. The document in question — a letter, to be frank — had been received by the personage robbed while alone in the royal *boudoir*. During its perusal she was suddenly interrupted by the entrance of the other exalted personage from whom specially it was her wish to conceal it. After a hurried and vain endeavour to thrust it in a drawer, she was forced to place it, open as it was, upon a table. The address, however, was uppermost, and, the contents thus unexposed, the letters escaped notice. At this juncture enters the Minister D—. His lynx eye immediately perceives the paper, recognises the handwriting of the address, observes the confusion of the personage addressed, and fathoms her secret. After some business transactions, hurried through in his ordinary manner, he produces a letter somewhat similar to the one in question, open it, pretends to read it, and then places it in close juxtaposition to the other. Again he converses, for some fifteen minutes, upon the public affairs. At length, in taking leave, he takes also from the table the letter to which he had no claim. Its rightful owner saw, but, of course, dared not call attention to the act, in the presence of the third personage who stood at her elbow. The minister decamped; leaving his own letter — one no importance - upon the table'.

'Here, then,' said Dupin to me, 'you have precisely what you demand to make the ascendancy complete — the robber's knowledge of the loser's knowledge of the robber.'

'Yes, replied the Prefect;' and the power does attained has, for some months past, been wielded, political purposes, to a very dangerous content. The personage robbed is more thoroughly convinced, everyday, of the necessity of reclaiming her letter. But this, of course, cannot be done openly. In fine, driven to despair, she has committed the matter to me.'

'Than whom,' said Dupin amid a perfect whirlwind of smoke, 'no more sagacious agent could, I suppose, be desired, or even imagined.'

'You flatter me,' replied the Prefect; 'but it is possible that some such opinion may have been entertained.'

'It is clear,' said I, 'as you observe, that the letter is still in possession of the minister; since it is this possession, and not any employment of the letter, which bestows the power. With the employment the power departs.

'True', said G.; 'and upon this conviction I proceeded. My first care was to make thorough search of the minister's hotel; and here my chief embarrassment lay in the necessity of searching without his knowledge. Beyond all things, I have been warned of the danger which would result from giving him reason to suspect our design.'

"But,' said I, 'you are quite *au fait* in these investigations. The Parisian police have done in this thing often before.'

'O yes; and for this reason I did not despair. The habits of the minister gave me, too, a great advantage. He is frequently absent from home all night. His servants are by no means numerous. They sleep at a distance from their master's apartment, and, being chiefly Neapolitans, are readily made drunk. I have keys, as you know, with which I can open any chamber or cabinet in Paris. For three months and night has not passed, during the greater part of which I have not been engaged, personally, in ransacking the D — Hotel. My honor is interested, and, to mention a great secret, the reward is enormous. So I did not abandon the search until I had become fully satisfied that the thief is a more astute man than myself. I fancy that I have investigated every nook and corner of the premises in which it is possible that the paper can be cancelled.'

'But it is not possible,' I suggested, 'that although the letter may be in possession of the minister, as it unquestionably is, he may have concealed it elsewhere than upon his own premises?'

'This is barely possible,' step Dupin. 'The present peculiar condition of affairs at court, and especially of those intrigues in which D- is known to be involved, would render the instant availability of the document- its susceptibility of being produced at a moment's notice - a point of nearly equal importance with its possession.'

'Its susceptibility of been produced?' said I.

'That is to say, of being destroyed,' said Dupin.

'True,' I observed; 'the paper is clearly then upon the premises. As for its being upon the person of the minister, we may consider that as out of the question.'

'Entirely,' said the Prefect. 'He have been twice waylaid, as if by footpads, and his person rigorously searched under my own inspection.'

'You might have spared yourself this trouble,' said Dupin. 'D — , I presume, is not altogether a fool, and, if not, must have anticipated these waylayings, as a matter of course.'

'Not altogether a fool,' said G., 'but then he's a poet, which I take to be only one remove from a fool.'

'True,' said Dupin, after a long and thoughtful whiff from his meerschaum, 'although I have been guilty of certain doggerel myself.'

'Suppose you detail,' said I, 'the particular of your search.'

'Why the fact is, we took our time, and we searched every where. I have had long experience in these affairs. I took the entire building, room my room; devoting the nights of a whole week to each. We examined, first, the furniture of each apartment. We opened every possible drawer; and I presume you know that, to be a properly trained police agent, such a thing as a secret drawer is impossible. Any man is a dolt permits a "secret" drawer to escape him in a search of this kind. The thing is so plain. There is a certain amount of bulk - of space - to be accounted for in every cabinet. Then we have accurate rules. The fiftieth part of a line could not escape us. After the cabinets we took the chairs. The cushions we probed with the fine long needles you have seen me employ. From the tables we removed the tops.'

'Why so?'

'Sometimes the top of a table, or other similarly arranged piece of furniture, is removed by the person wishing to conceal an article; then the leg is excavated, the article deposited within the cavity, and the top replaced. The bottoms and tops of bed-posts are employed in the same way.'

'But could not the cavity be detected by sounding?' I asked.

'By no means, if, when the article is deposited, a sufficient wadding of cotton be placed around it. Besides, in our case, we were obliged to proceed without noise.'

But you could not have removed - you could not have taken to piece all article of furniture in which it would have been possible to make a deposit in the manner you mention. A letter may be compressed into a thin spiral roll, not differing much in shape or bulk from a large knitting-needle, and in this form it might be inserted into the rung of a chair, for example,'You did not take to a pieces all the chairs?'

'Certainly not; But we did it is better-we examined the rungs of every chair in the hotel, and indeed, the joints of every description of furniture, by the aid of a most powerful microscope. Had there been any traces of recent disturbance we should not have failed to detect it instantly. A single grain of gimlet dust, for example, would have been obvious as an apple. Any disorder in the glueing—any unusual gaping in the joints—would have sufficed to insure protection.'

'I presume you looked to the mirrors, between the boards and the plate, and you probed the beds and the bed-clothes, as well as the curtains and carpets.'

'That of course; and when we had absolutely completed every particle of the furniture in this way, then we examined the house itself. We divided its entire surface into compartments, which we numbered, so that none might be missed; then we scrutinized each individual square inch throughout the premises, including the two houses immediately adjoining, with the microscope, as before.'

'The two houses adjoining!' I exclaimed; 'you must have had a great deal of trouble.'

'We had; but the reward offered in prodigious.'

'You include the grounds about the houses?'

'All the grounds are paved with brick. They gave us comparatively little trouble. We examined the moss between the bricks, and found it undisturbed.'

'You looked among D-'s papers, of course, and into the books of the library?'

'Certainly : we opened every package and parcel; we not only opened every book, but we turned over every leaf in each volume, not contenting ourselves with a mere shake, according to the fashion of some of our police officers. We also measured the thickness of every book cover, with the most accurate admeasurement, and applied to each the most jealous scrutiny of the microscope. Had any of the bindings been recently meddled with it would have been utterly impossible that the fact should have escaped observation. Some five or six volumes, just from the hands of the binder, we carefully probed, longitudinally, with the needles.'

'You explored the floors beneath the carpets?'

'Beyond doubt. We removed every carpet, and examined the boards with the microscope.'

'And the paper on the walls?'

'Yes.'

'You looked into the cellars?'

'We did.'

'Then,' I said, 'you have been making a miscalculation, and the letter in not upon the premises, as you suppose.'

'I fear you are right there,' said the Prefect. 'And now, Dupin, what would you advise me to do?'

'To make a thorough research of the premises.'

'That is absolutely needless,' replied G- 'I am not more sure that I breathe than I am that the letter is not at the Hotel.'

'I have no better advice to give you,' said Dupin. 'You have of course, an accurate description of the letter?'

'Oh yes!'—And here the Prefect, producing a memorandum-book, proceeded to read aloud a minute account of the internal, and especially of the external appearance of the missing document. Soon after finishing the perusal of this description, he took his departure, more entirely depressed in spirits than I had ever known good gentleman before.

In about a month afterwards he paid us another visit, and found us occupied very nearly as before. He took a pipe and a chair and entered into some ordinary conversation. At length I said,-

Well, but G—, what of the purloined letter? I presume you have at last made up your mind that there is no such thing as overreaching the Minister?'

'Confound him, say I—yes; I made the re-examination, however, as Dupin suggested- but it was all labor lost, as I knew it would be.'

'How much was the reward offered, did you say?' asked Dupin.

'Why, very a great deal—a very liberal award I don't like to say how much, precisely; but one thing I will say, that I wouldn't mind giving my individual check for fifty thousand Francs to any one who could obtain me that letter. The fact is, it is becoming of more and more important everyday; and the reward has been later doubled. If it were trebled, however, I could do no more than I have done.'

'Why, yes,' said Dupin, drawlingly, between the whiffs of his meerschaum, 'I really-think, G—, you have not exerted your-self—to the uttermost in this matter. You might—do a little more, I think, eh.'

'How?- in what way ?'

'Why-puff, puff,-you might-puff, puff -employ-counsel in the matter, eh? — puff, puff, puff. Do you remember the story they tell of Abernethy?'

'No; hang Abernethy!'

To be sure! Hang him and welcome. But, once upon a time, a certain rich miser conceived the design of spunging upon this Abernethy for a medical opinion. Getting up, for this purpose, and ordinary conservation in a private company, he insinuated his case to the physician, as that of of an imaginary individual "We will suppose," state the miser, "that these symptoms are such and such; now, doctor, what would you have directed him to take"" "Take!" said Abernethy, "why, take advice, to be sure."

'But,' said the Prefect, a little discomposed, 'I am perfectly willing to take advice, and to pay for it. I would really give fifty thousand francs to anyone who would aid me in the matter.'

'In the case,' is applied Dupin, opening a drawer, and producing a check-book, 'you may as well fill me up a check for the amount mentioned. When you have signed it, I will hand you the letter.'

I was astounded. The Prefect appeared absolutely thunder-stricken. For some minutes he remained speechless and motionless, looking incredulously at my friend with open mouth, and eyes that seems starting from their socket; then, apparently recovering himself in some measure, he seized a pen, and after several pauses and vacant stares, finally filled up and signed a check for fifty thousand francs, and handed it across the table to Dupin. The latter examined it carefully and deposited it in his pocket-book; then, unlocking an *escritorire*, took thence a letter and gave it to the Prefect. This functionary grasped it in a perfect agony of joy, opened it with a trembling hand, cast of rapid glance at its contents, and then, scrambling and struggling to the door, rushed at length unceremoniously from the room and from the house, without having uttered a syllable since Dupin had requested him to fill up the check. When he had gone, my friend entered into some explanation.

'The Parisian police,' he said, 'are exceedingly table in their way. They are preserving, ingenious, cunning, and thoroughly versed in the knowledge which duties seen chiefly to demand. Thus, when G- detailed to us his mode of searching the premises at the Hotel D-, I felt entire confidence in his having made a satisfactory investigation—so far as his labors extended.

'So far as his labour extended?' said I.

'Yes,' said Dupin. 'The measures adopted were not only the best of their kind, but carried out to absolute perfection. Had the letter been deposited within the range of their search, these fellows would, beyond a question, have found it.

I merely laughed—but he seemed quite serious in all that he said. 'The measures then,' he continued, 'were good in their kind, and well executed; their defect lay in their being inapplicable to the case, and to the man. A certain set of highly ingenious resources are, with the Prefect, a sort of Procrustean bed, to which he forcibly adapted his design. But he perpetually errs by being too deep or too shallow, for the matter in hand; and many a school boy is a better reasoner than he. I knew one about eight year of age, whose success at guessing in the game of "even and odd" attracted universal admiration. This game is simple, and is played with Marbles. One player holds in his hand a number of these toys, and demanded of another whether that number is even or odd. If the guess is right the guesser win one; if wrong, he lose one. The boy to whom I allude won all the Marbles of the school. Of course had some principle of guessing; and display in this lay mere observation and admeasurement of the astuteness of his opponents. For example, an arrant simpleton in his opponent, and, holding up his closed hand, asks "are they are they even or odd?' Our schoolboy replies, "odd." and loses; but upon the second trial he wins, for he then say to himself, "the simpleton had them even upon the first trial, and his amount of cunning is just sufficient to make him have them odd upon the second; I will therefore guess odd;"-he guesses odd, and wins. Now, with a simpleton a degree above the first, he would have reasoned thus: "This fellow finds that in the first instance I guessed odd, and, in the second, he will propose to himself upon the first impulse, a simple variation from even to odd, as did the first simpleton; but then a second thought will suggest that this is too simple a variation, and finally he will decide upon putting it even as before. I will therefore get even"- he guesses even, and wins. Now this mode of reasoning in the schoolboy, whom his fellow termed "lucky,"- what, in its last analysis, 'It is nearly,' I said, 'an identification of reasoner's intellect with that of his opponent.'

'It is,' said Dupin; 'and, upon inquiring of the boy by what means he effected the thorough identification in which his success consisted, I received answer as follow: "When I wish to find out how wise to find out how wise, or how stupid, or how good, or how wicked is any one, or what are his thoughts at the moment, I fashion the expression of my face, as accurately as possible, in accordance with the expression of his, and then wait to see what thoughts or sentiments in my mind or heart, as if to match or correspond with the expression." This response of the schoolboy lies at the bottom of all the spurious profundity which has been attributed to Rochfoucauld, to La Bougive, to Machiavelli, and Campanella.

'And the identification,' I said, of the reasoner's intellect with that of his opponent, defends, if I understand you aright, upon the accuracy with which the opponent's intellect is admeasured.'

'For its practical value it depends upon this,' replied Dupin; 'and the Prefect and his cohort want fail so frequently, first, by default of his identification, and, secondly by ill-measurement, or rather through non-measurement, of the intellect with which they are engaged. They consider only their own ideas of intensity; and, in searching for anything hidden, advert only to the modes in which they would have hidden it. They are right in this much—that their own ingenuity is a faithful representative of that of the *mass*; but when the cunning of the individual felon is diverse in character from their own, the felon foils them, of course. This always happens when it is above their own, and very usually when it is blow. They have no variation of the principle in their investigation; and best, when urged, by some unusual emergency—by some extraordinary reward—they extend or exaggerate their for modes of practice, without touching their principles. What, for example in this case of D—, has been done to vary the principle of action? What is all this boring, and probing, and sounding, and scrutinizing with the microscope, and dividing the surface of the building into the registered square inches— what is it all but an exaggeration of the application of the one principal or set of principle of search, which are based upon the one set of notions regarding human ingenuity, which the Prefect, in the long routine of his duty, has been accustomed? Do you not see he has taken it for granted that all men proceed to cancel a letter,— not exactly in a gimlet-hole bored in chair leg—but, at least, in some out of the way hole or corner suggested by the same tenor of thought which would urge a man to a secrete a letter in a gimlet-hole bored in the chair leg? And do you not see also, that such *recherches* nooks for concealment are adapted only for ordinary occasions, and would be adopted only by ordinary intellects; for, in all cases of concealment, a disposal of the articles concealed—a disposal of it in this *recherche* manner,—is, in the very first instance, presumable and presumed; and thus its discovery depends, not at all upon the acumen, but altogether upon the mere care, patience, and determination of the seekers; and where the case is of importance—or, what amounts to be the same thing in the political eyes, when the reward is of magnitude,—the qualities in question have never been known to fail.

You will now understand what I meant in suggesting that, had the purloined letter been hidden anywhere within the limits of the Prefect's examination—in other words, had the principal of it concealment been comprehended within the principles of the Prefect—its discovery would have been a matter altogether beyond question. This functionary, however, has been thoroughly mystified; and the remote source of his defeat lies in the supposition that the Minister is a fool, because he has acquired read renown as a poet. All fools are poets; this the Prefect feels; and he is merely guilty of a non *distributio medii* in thence inferring that all poets are fools.

'But is it really the poet?' I asked. 'There are two brothers, I know; and both have attained reputation in letters. The Minister I believe has written learnedly on the Differential Calculus. He is mathematician, and no poet.'

'You are mistaken; I know him well; he is both. As poet and mathematician, he would reason well; as mathematician, he could not have reasoned at all, and thus would have been at the mercy of the Prefect.'

'You surprise me,' I said, 'by these opinions, which have been contradicted by the voice of the world. You do not mean to set at naught the well-digested idea of centuries. The mathematical reason has long been regarded as the reason *par excellence.*'

"'Il y a a parier.'" replied Dupin, quoting from Chamfort, "*que toute idee publique, toute convention recue, est une sottise, car elle a convenu au plus grand nombre.*" The mathematicians, I grant you, have done their best to get the popular error to which you allude, and which is nonetheless an error for its promulgation as truth. With an art worthy a better cause, for example, they have insinuated the term "analysis" into application to algebra. The French are the originators of this particular deception; but if a term is of any importance—if words derive any value from applicability—then "analysis" conveys "algebra" about much as, in Latin, *"ambitus"* implies "ambition," *"religio"* "religion," or *"homines honesti."* a set of *honorable* men.

'You have a quarrel on hand, I see,' said I, 'with some of the algebraists of Paris; but proceed.'

'I dispute the availability, and thus the value, of that reason which is cultivated in any especial form other than the abstractly logical. I dispute, in particular, the reason educed by mathematical reasoning is merely logic applied to observation upon form and quantity. The great error lies is supposing that even the truths of what is called *pure* algebra, are abstract or general truths. And this error is so egregious that I am confounded at the universality with which it has been received. Mathematical axioms are not axioms of general truth. What is true of *relation*—of form and quantity—is often grossly false in regard to morals, for example. In this latter science it is very usually *untrue* that the aggregated parts are equal to the whole. In chemistry also the axiom fails. In the consideration of motive it fails; for two motives, each of a given value, have not, necessarily, a value when united, equal to the sum of their values apart. There are numerous other mathematical argues, from his *finite truths*, through habit, as if they were of an absolutely general applicability - as the world indeed imagines them to be. Bryant, in his very learned "Mythology," mentions an analogous source of error, when he says that "although the Pagan fables are not believed, yet we forget ourselves continually, and make inferences from them as existing realities." With the *algebraists*, however, who are Pagans themselves, the "Pagan fables" are believed, and the inferences are made, not so much are made not so much through lapse of memory, as through an unacccountable addling of the brains. In short, I never yet encountered the mere mathematician who could be trusted out of equal roots, or one who did not clandestinely hold it as a point of his faith that X2 + px was absolutely and unconditionally equal to *q*. Say to one of these gentlemen, by way of experiment, if you please, that you believe optionally occasions may occur where x2 + px is not altogether equal to q, and, having made him understand what you mean, to get out of his reach as speedily as convenient, for, beyond doubt, he will endeavour to knock you down.

'I mean to say,' continue Dupin, while I am merely laughed at his last observation, 'that if the Minister had been no more than a mathematician, the Prefect would have been under no necessity of giving need this check. I knew him, however, as both mathematician and poet, and my measures were adapted to his capacity, with reference to the circumstances by which he was surrounded. I knew him as a courtier, too, and as a bold *intrigant*. Such a man, I considered, could not fail to be aware of the ordinary political modes of action. He could not have failed to anticipate—and events have proved that he did not fail to anticipate—the waylaying's to which he was subjected. He must have foreseen, I reflected the secret investigation of his premises. His frequent absences from home at night, which were hailed by the Prefect as certain aids to his success, I regarded only as ruses, to afford opportunity for thorough search to the police, and thus the sooner impress them with the conviction to which G—, did finally arrive the conviction that the letter was not upon the premises. I felt, also, that the whole train of thought, which I was at some action, in searches for articles concealed— I felt that this whole train of thought would necessarily pass through the mind of the Minister. It would imperatively lead him to despise all the ordinary *nooks* of concealment. He could not, I reflected, be so weak as not to see that the most intricate and remote recess of his Hotel would be as open as his commonest closet to the eyes, to the probes, to the gimlets and to the microscopes of the Prefect.

I saw, in fine, that he would be driven, as a matter of course, to simplicity, if not deliberately induced it to as a matter of choose. You will remember, perhaps, how desperately the Prefect laughed when I suggested, upon our first interview, that it was just possible this mystery troubled him so much on account of its being so very self-evident.'

'Yes,' I, said I, 'I remember his merriment well. I really thought he would have fallen into convulsions.

The material world,' continued Dupin, 'abound with very strict analogies to the immaterial; and thus some color of both has been given to the rhetorical dogma, that metaphor, or simile, may be made to strengthen an argument, as well as to embellish a description. The principle of the *vis inertiae*, for example, seems to be identical in physics and metaphysics. It is not more to the former, that a large body is with more difficulty set in motion than a smaller one, and that its *subsequent momentum* is commensurate with this difficulty, than it is, in the latter that intellect off the vaster capacity, while more forcible, more constant, and more eventful in their movements than those of inferior grade, are yet the left readily moved, and more embarrassed and full of hesitation in the first few steps of their progress. Again: have you ever noticed which of the street signs, over the shop doors, are the most attractive of attention?'

'I have never given the matter thought,' I said.

'There is a game of puzzles,' he resumed, 'which is played upon a map. One party requires another to find a given word—the name of the town, river, state or empire—any word, in short, upon the motley and perplexed surface of the chart. A novice in the game generally seeks to embarrass his opponents by giving them the most minutely lettered names; but the adept selects such words as stretch, in large characters, from one end of the chart to the other. These, like the over-largely lettered signs and placards of the street, escape observation by dint of be excessively obvious; and here the physical oversight is precisely analogous with the moral in apprehension by which the intellect suffers to pass unnoticed those consideration which are too obtrusively and too palpably self-evident. But this is a point, it appears, somewhat above or beneath the understanding of the Prefect. He never once thought it probable, or possible, that the Minister had deposited the letter immediately beneath the nose of the whole world, by way of the best preventing any portion of that world from perceiving it.

'But the more I reflected upon the daring, dashing, and discriminating ingenuity of D-; upon the fact that the document must always have been at hand, if he intended to use it to good purpose; and upon the decisive evidence, obtained by the Perfect, that it was not hidden within the limits of that dignitary's ordinary's search—the more satisfied I became that, to conceal this letter, the Minister had restored to the comprehensive the sagacious expedient of not attempting to conceal it at all.

'Full of these idea, I prepared myself with a pair of green spectacles, and called one fine morning, quite by accident, at the Ministerial hotel. I found D—at home, yawning, lounging, and drawdling, as usual, and pretending to be in the last extremity of ennui. He is perhaps, the most really energetic human being now alive—but that is the only when nobody see him.

'To be even with him, I complained of my awake eyes, and lamented the necessity of the spectacles, under cover of which I cautiously and thoroughly surveyed the apartment, while seemingly intent only upon conversation of my post.

'I paid special attention to a large writing-table near which he sat, and upon which they confusedly, some miscellaneous letters and other papers, with one or two musical instruments and a few books. Here, however, after a long and very deliberate scrutiny, I saw nothing to excite particular suspicion.

At length my eyes, in going the circuit of the room, fell upon a trumpery fill agree card-rack of pasteboard, that hung dangling by a dirty blue ribbon, from a little brass knob just beneath the middle of the metalpiece. In this rack, which had three or four compartments, were five- six visiting cards and solitary letter. This last was much soiled and crumpled. It was torn nearly in two, across the middle—as if a design, in the first instance, to tear it entirely up as worthless, had been altered, or stayed, in the second. It had a large black seal, bearing the D— cipher *very* conspicuously, and was addressed, in a diminutive female hand to D—, the minister, himself. It was thrust carelessly, and even, as it seemed, contemptuously, into one of the upper division of the rack. 'No sooner had I glanced at this letter, than I concluded it to be that of which I was in search. To be sure, it was, to all appearances, radically different from the one of which the Prefect had read us so a minute description. Here the seal was large and black, with the D- cipher, there it was small and red, with ducal arms of the S- family. Here the address, to the Minister, was diminutive and feminine, there the superscription, to a certain Royal personage, was markedly bold and decided; the size alone formed a point of correspondence. But, then, the radicalness of these differences, which was excessive; the dirt; the soiled and the torn condition of the paper, so inconsistent with the true methodical habit of D-, and so suggestive of a design to delude the beholder into an idea of the worthlessness of the document; these things, together with the hyper obtrusive of this document, full in the view of every visitor, and thus exactly in accordance with the conclusions to which I had previously arrived; these things, I say, was strongly corroborative of suspicions, in one who came up with the intention to suspect.

'I protracted my visit as long as possible, and, I while I maintained a most emanated discussion with the Minister, on a topic which I knew well had never failed to interest and excite him, I kept my attention really riveted upon the letter. In this examination, I committed to memory its external appearance and arrangement in the rack; and also fell, at length, upon a discovery which set at rest whatever trivial doubt I am might have entertained. In scrutinizing the edge of the paper, I observed them to be more chafed then seemed necessary. They presented the broken appearances which is manifested when a stiff paper, having been folded and pressed with a folder, is refolded in a reserved direction, in the same creases or edges which had formed the original fold. This discovery was sufficient. It was clear to me that the latter had been turned, as a glove, inside out, re-directed, and re-sealed. I bade the Minister good morning, and took my departure at once, leaving a gold snuff-box up on the table.

The next morning I called for the snuff-box, when we resumed, quite eagerly, the conversation of the preceding day. While thus engaged however, a loud report, as if of a pistol, was heard immediately beneath the windows of the hotel, and was succeeded by a series of fearful screams, and the shouting of the mob. D- rushed to a casement, threw it open, and looked out. In the meantime, I stepped to the card-track, took the letter, put in my pocket, and replace it by a facsimile, (so far as regard externals,) which I had carefully prepared at my lodgings; imitating the D- cipher, very readily, by means of a seal forward the bread.

'The disturbance in the street had been occasioned by the frantic behaviour of a man with the musket. He had fired it among a crowd of a women and children. It proved, however, to have been without ball, and the fellow was suffered to go his way as an lunatic or a drunkard. When he had gone, D- came from the window, whither I had followed him immediately with upon securing the object in view. Soon afterward I bade him farewell. The pretended lunatic was a man in my own pay.'

'But what purpose had you,' I asked, in replacing the letter by a facsimile? Would it not have been better, at the first visit, to have seized it openly, and departed?'

'D-,' replied Dupin, is a desperate man, and a man of nerve. His hotel, too, is not without attendants devoted to his interests. Had I made the wide at attempt you suggest, I might never have left the Ministerial presence alive. The good people of Paris might have heard of me no more. But I had an object apart from these considerations. You know my political prepossessions. In this matter, I act as a partisan of the lady concerned. For eighteen months the Minister has had her in his power. She has now him in hers; since, being unaware that the letter is not in his possession, he will proceed with his exactions as if it was. Thus will he inevitably commit himself, at once, to his political destruction. His downfall, too, will not be more precipitate than awkward. It is all very well to talk about the facilis descensus Averni; but in all kinds of climbing, as Catalani said of singing, it is far more easy to get up than to come down. In the present instance I have no sympathy—at least no pity for him who descends. He is that monstrum horrendum, an unprincipled man of genius. I confess, however, that I should like very well to know the precise character of his thoughts, when, being defied by her whom the Prefect terms "a certain personage," he is reduced to opening the letter which I felt for him in the card-rack.'

'How? did you put any thing particular in it?

'Why-it did not seem altogether right to leave the interior blank- that would have been insulting D-, at Vienna once, did me an evil turn, which I told him, quite good-humoredly, that I should remember. So, as I knew he would feel some curiosity in regard to the identity of the person who had outwitted him, I thought it a pity not to give him a clue. He is well acquainted with my MS., and I just copied into the middle of the blank sheet the words-

—Un dessein si funeste,

Sil n'est digne d'Atree, est digne de Thyete.

They are to be found in Crebillon's "Atree."

• • • •

Word Notes and Annotations

Nil Sapientiae odiosius acumine nimio—Seneca

This Latin sentence is attributed to Seneca. Poe used this sentence in his 1845 second edition of The Purloined Letter. The meaning of this Latin sentence is 'Nothing is more abominable to wisdom than excessive cunning.'

Gusty- Sudden violent condition of the wind, rain, smoke and even temper.

Two fold Luxury- Double comfort.

Meerschaum—Tobacco pipe with bowl made from this.

C. Auguste Dupin—(N) Name of the private detective. According to some critic, he is the predecessor of Sherlock Holmes; he is the immortal creation of Edgar Allan Poe, the father of detective story. Poe featured C. Auguste Dupin in the stories like The Murders in the Rue Morgue, The Mystery of Marie Roget etc.

au troisieme—Third floor

Curling eddies—ringlets of circular smokes.

Affair of the Rue Morgue—Bloodsheds and murders in the story The Murders in the Rue Morgue by Poe.

Prefect—Chief administrative officer in District of France.

That is another of your odd notions-—The Parisian police Prefect G— has an uncanny habit of saying 'odd' everything which is beyond his knowledge.

Excessively odd — Extremely abnormal

Baffles — perplexes or bewilders

You will be the death of me yet— You will be the cause of my death. You'll be responsible for my death.

Contemplative — of Contemplation/Meditative

Last importance — Extreme importance

Puff — Short, quick breadth.

Purloined — Lost

Royal apartments — Majestic rooms

Inferred — Deduced or derived

Explicit — Clear or categorical

Verture — Expose to risk

Exalted — Made lofty or noble

Ascendancy — Dominant control

Jeopardised — Endangered

Ingenious — Artful/clever at contriving

Boudoir — Woman's private room

Lynx — Wild Cat with keen eyesight

Fathoms — Comprehends; measures the depth

Juxtaposition — Side by side

Decamped — Departed suddenly

("Here then ... under my own inspection)

Wielded — Exerted

Whirlwind — Vortex, very rapid

Sagacious — Showing good judgement

au fait —Third floor

Neapolitans — Native of Naples

Ransacking — Thoroughly searching

Astute — Shrewed

Every nook and corner — Every where

Intrigues — Underhand plots

Susceptibility — Vulnerability

Waylaid — Stopped to rob; accosted

(You might here ... a great deal of trouble)

Anticipated death — with before proper time.
Whiff — Puff of air or smoke
Doggerel — Insignificant poem
Dolt — Stupid
Excavated — Reveal or extract by digging
Wadding — Filling, padding
Rung — Step of ladder
Gimlet dust — Dust from the boring tool

("We had; but ... as I knew it would be")

Prodigious — Marvellous
Meddled with — Interfered in other's concerns
Cellars — Underground storage room; wine cellars
Memorandum book — Book with notes or records for future use.
Confound — Baffle; confuse

**(How much was the reward ...
so far as his labors extended?" said I)**

Francs — French currency
Trebled — Three fold; triple
Drawlingly — Speaking with drawn out vowel sound.
Exerted — Gave effort; struggled
Insinuated — Hinted obliquely
Astounded — Astonished
Incredulously — Suspiciously
Escritoire — Writing desk with drawers
Unceremoniously — Abruptly

("Yes". Said Dupin ... opponent's intellect is admeasured)

Procrustean — Enforcing uniformity without regard to natural variation
Allude — hint at
Astuteness — Shrewdness

Arrant Simpleton — Utter stupid
Profundity — Erudition
Rochefoucauld — French writer of moralistic maxims.
La Bougive — Higher class people (French)
Machiavelli — Italian philosopher
Campanella — Little bell (Italian)

("For its practical value ... algebraists of Paris; but proceed")

Cohort — one tenth of Roman legion
Felon — One who has committed violent crime
Gimlet -hole — Hole made by boring tool.
Recherches — Far fetched
Acumen — Keen insight
Non Distribulio medii — Fallacy of the undistributed middle (Latin)
Chamfort — Nicholas Chamfort, French writer
(que toute idee puflique, toute convention recue, est une sottise, car eue a convenu an plus grand nombre)
Promulgate — Proclaim

("I dispute the availability ... most attractive of attention?")

Egrerious — Extremely bad
Axioms — Established principles
Pagan — Headline ; non-believers of Christianity
Chandestinely — Secretly
Intriguant — Intriguer
Embelish — Decorate

("I have never given ... intention to suspeet)

Novice — Beginner
Seemingly — Doubtfully
Trumpeny — Rubbish; Showy but worthless

Filigree — Fine ornamental work in gold.
Dangling — Hanging loosely
Diminutive — Tiny
Cipher — Secret writing
Inconsistent — Variable
Delude — Deceive; mistead
Corroborative — Supportive.

("I profracted my visit ... in Crebillon's Atree")

Protracted — Drawn-out
Riveted — Fastened with rivets
Snuff box — Box putting powdered tobacco etc.
Facsimile — Exact copy of writing
Musket — Light gun
Frantic — Wildly excited
Partisan — Strong supporter of party, side etc.
Precipitate — Accelerate

Abernethy — C. Auguste Dupin narrates the story of Abernethy regarding medical advice. A rich miser once met Mr. Abernethy and told him about an imaginary individual regarding his physical problems. Then that miser asked Mr. Abernethy to suggest any cure for those physical symptoms that were really of his own. Mr. Abernethy then advised to take advice.

"*Il Y a a parier, aue toute idee publique, toute convention recue, est une Sottise, car elle or convenn au plus frand nombre*"

You can bet on the fact that an idea and convention that is widely accepted is wrong, for it is simply convenient to the greater mumber. (Chamfort's Maximes et Pensees)

Un dessein Si funeste, il ri'est digne d'Atree, est digue de Thyeste.

This sentence is quoted from Crefillon's Atree. It means. "So infamous a schem If not worthy of Atreus, Is worthy of Thystes".

Facilis descersus Averno —

This Latin phrase means "The descent to hell is easy".

Procrustean bed —

In Greek mythology, there was a ferocious giant named Procrustes. He used to capture human beings and then stretch or cut off the limbs according to the length of his bed.

Critical Summary of The Purloined Letter

C. Auguste Dupin, the Parisian private detective and his partner, the unnamed narrator, were discussing over the incident in their case study of The Murder in the Rue Morgue. They are joined by Mr. G —, the Parisian police Prefect who has a case to discuss with the detective. The Prefect went on with the details of the case which, in his opinion, "is very simple indeed" but at the same time "so excessively odd."

Once the Queen was reading a personal and intimate letter from her friend in her boudoir. She was interrupted by the King and Queen hurriedly put the letter on the table. In the meantime Minister D — entered into the room for some important business, looked the letter, recognised the handwriting, and cunningly exchanged with one of his letter that had no importance. The Queen could not say anything in the fear that her affair will be known to the King who was standing "on her elbow". The Minister's attitude was sinister and he was blackmailing the Queen for his political benefit. The police Prefect made two inferences which Mr. Dupin agrees with:

(i) The contents of the letter have not been revealed and the letter is still with the Minister D —.

(ii) The letter is very much important, so Minister kept the letter close at hand.

Then the Prefect went on saying how they searched for the letter in the Minister D —'s house and found nothing. Mr. G— with his police team made a thorough search in the hotel of Mr. D — . It was a very difficult task to perform. They carried out this search at night as the minister does not stay at night in the hotel. Mr. G — has had all the duplicate keys with him. So it was not difficult for him to open all the rooms of the house. During the search, the police took the entire building room by room and devoted themselves the nights of a whole week. They thoroughly examined the furniture, they opened all the secret drawers, they examined every cabinet, they probed the cushions with fine long needles and they also removed the top of the tables to find if there were any excavated holes to conceal the letter.

They also examined the chairs and other furniture with a powerful microscope to find any trace of disorders in gluing. They examined every inch of the house including outer area of the premises; they examined all the books in the library; they probed into the floors beneath the carpet and even the cellars. But all their endeavours went in vein. The letter was not found anywhere .

So the Prefect came to visit Mr. Dupin to have some ideas regarding the solution of the mystery. Mr. Dupin listened to all the methods applied by the Paris police and he advised Mr. G — to "make a thorough research of the premises" and also wanted to know the description of the letter. The Prefect gave him the minute details of the purloined letter and left the room in despair.

After one month, the Prefect visited C. Auguste Dupin again. He was looking very hopeless in spite of the fact that a large amount of reward was declared for the letter. He assumed that anyone who could retrieve the purloined letter would get a cheque of fifty thousand Francs. Mr. Dupin told him to write the cheque and assured him to produce the letter instantly. The Prefect became almost dumb in wonder, wrote the cheque and received letter and left the room quickly to deliver the letter to its original owner, the Queen.

Then Mr. Dupin explained how he retrieved the purloined letter from the hands of powerful Minister D —.

He opined that the Paris police were undoubtedly competent with their methodical investigation. But what they lacked was common sense. There method was so conventional that they could not understand the depth of wisdom in The Minister's mind. However, he gives an anecdote of a clever boy who won all the marbles from his opponent players in the game called "even and odd". The boy was so intelligent that he could read the mind of his opponent and use his common sense to guess the number whether it was even or odd. Dupin used the same trick to find out the letter. He made a visit to the Minister's apartment. He wore a pair of green spectacles and complained about his weak eyesight. While discussing on a topic with the Minister, he secretly noticed the room and he eyed a "ripped letter, much soiled and crumpled and suspending on a rack beneath the mantle-piece. The letter was kept open and its corners were chaffed in such a way that none can have least doubt about its importance. Being assumed regarding the purloined letter, Dupin bade goodbye to the Minister learning his golden snuff-box on the table so that he can visit again the Minister's house.

The next day Dupin returned on the pretence of taking his snuff-box back. According to his pre-planned setting, a man behaved frantically with a musket in his hand and "fired it among a crowd of women and children". It was arranged to attract the attention of the Minister on the street and in the meantime, Dupin switched the letter on the mantle with a facsimile of his own handwriting. He did it very carefully and craftily. Otherwise, "the good people of Paris might have heard of me no more." The Minister was a desperate man, a man of nerve. Once he offended Mr. Dupin at Vienna. Dupin now took his revenge by the letter thus enhancing the political ruin of the Minister who, with his "political prepossessions", will continue his intrigue against the Queen and will hasten his downfall. Dupin inscribed in the middle of the fascimile : "un dessin Si funste, Sil n est digne d ' Atree, est digne de Thystes," meaning — a sinister scheme, if it is not worth of Atreus, is worthy of Thystes.

Critical Commentary on The Purloined Letter

The story begins with a single-lined epigraph "Nihil Sapientiae Odiosius acumine nimio" which means nothing is more scornful to wisdom than excessive cleverness. This Latin line is attributed to Seneca by Poe but with such a sentence was never found in Senecan works. It is rather found in Petrarch's treatise "De Remedies utriusane Fortunae".

However, The Purloined Letter remains as the best detective story written by Poe and it establishes a new tradition in the detective genre by turning away from action towards intellectual analysis for solving the mystery. In his earlier story The Murder in the Rue Morgue, Poe used graphic violence i.e. bodily mutilation and almost decapitation by a wild animal. But in The Purloined Letter he shunned this gory crime of passion and the writer employed a simple mystery whose solution is hidden in an open place.

In these two stories, namely The Murder in the Rue Morgue and The Purloined Letter, two different attitudies of C. Auguste Dupin are revealed. In The Rue Morgue, Dupin took up the case as a challenge and amusement but not for any financial benefit. He showed cent percent amateurish attitude. But in case of The Purloined Letter, Dupin takes up the case for two-fold reason. The first one is financial gain and the other is personal revenge upon the Minister D— who once offended him in Vienna. We don't know what was the nature of offence made by the Minister, but Dupin could not forget it and when the moment of revenge turned up unexpectedly, he grabbed it instantly. Here we find Dupin's innovative method to solve the mystery by trying to identify the psychology of the criminal i.e. the Minister D— Both Mr. Dupin and the Minister were acquainted to each other, both had skills in mathematics and poetry and their clash of wits is threatened to end in deadlock. But at the end of the struggle, Dupin wins the game as he is morally superior to his opponent who is blackmailer, who is a morally unprincipled and wants to enjoy power by exploiting the weakness of others.

In The Purloined Letter unlike other detective stories of Poe such as The Murder in The Rue Morgue or The Mystery of the Mary Roger, action and violence has been replaced by intelligence, reflectiveness and the study of the human psychology. That is why the setting of The Purloined Letter has been shifted from the city streets of The Rue Morge or the wide outdoors of Mary Roger to an enclosed private library room where the narrator and Dupin are engaged in discussing ideas and most of the actions of the story are passed on by flashback technique.

The story begins with the narrator and Dupin's dispassionate rumination of the past which takes a turn after the arrival of the police Prefect in Dupin's library. The Prefect is a man of active nature with unreflective character. He is a Prefect police Prefect to carry out his investigation on his linear methodical ways, but he lacks the depth in the human psychology. Dupin also criticises him for his robotic way of investigation. He sets a standard procedure for inspection, and sticks to that track till the end and never tries to read the minds of the criminals who commit the crimes and baffle the police with their evil genius. On the other hand, Dupin plays with the sub-conscious of the cultprit; he employs "even and odd" theory in the game of guessing and ultimately win the race.

Immediately after hearing the story of The Purloined Letter, Dupin sketched the situation in his mind and resolved to retrieve the letter from the Minister although he never showed any sign of such resolution, nor he made the Prefect feel that he had an undercurrent of revenge against the Minister who once offended him in Vienna. We get a hint of this revengeful rivalry between Minister D — and C. Auguste Dupin from the inscription inside his facsimile letter — 'Un dessein Si funeste, S'il ri' est digue d' Atree, est digne de Thyeste' meaning "a Scheme So Scornful, if is not worthy of Atreus, is worthy of Thyestes". Dupin cited this line from the French dramatist Crebillon's tragic play Atree 'est Thyeste (Atreus and Thyestes). Atreus and Thyeste were two brothers. Thyeste seduced wife of Atreus. To take revenge upon his brother, Atreus killed the sons of Thyestes and served their meat to him at feast. Atreus' act is considered as legitimate as its repays the original offence of the brother. Dupin also justifies his act of befooling the Minister and taking the letter in his custody as the Prefect revenge from Atreus.

The story of the Purloined Letter is based on two similar incidents — one is the purloining of a personal letter by the Minister D —, and other is the retrieving of the letter by the detective Dupin with a 'Tit for Tat' style. The owner of the letter, a lady with the royal dignity was studying the letter secretly in her boudoir. Hardly she finished reading than her husband entered into the room and she hurriedly kept the letter on the table. It is evident from this incident that the lady had an affair with a third person whose identity remains closed throughout the story. And it is quite sure that her husband was not aware about that secret affair. In the meantime, Minister D — entered into the room for an urgent business, found the letter on the table quite open, recognised the handwriting on the envelope and craftily exchanged that letter with an unimportant one. The royal lady could not protest and his husband was standing near her elbow. If she spoke a word, her secret affair was sure to be public and her royal dignity and honour could be at stake. Minister D — took advantage of that crisis moment and later blackmailed the queen for his political benefit. The queen then engaged Mr. G, the Prefect of the Paris police, to find out the letter and she also declared a lucrative prize if the letter was handed over to her. Mr. G — employed all his professional knowledge, investigated the Minister's apartment at night in his absence, searched every inch of the rooms in the apartment in his unmistaken methodical way, but failed to retrieve the letter. Then he met with Mr. Dupin, the amateur detective, if he could give him some clue regarding the purloined letter.

Poe's narrative technique or weaving the plot is marvelous in this story. Nothing happens directly in the story. We only get flashback narratives of all the incidents. Dupin now comes into action. He considered the Minister a man of superior intelligence, rather cunning and crook. Dupin once met with the Minister in disguise at his apartment. He wore a pair as green spectacles and told that he had been suffering from ocular problems. He conversed with the Minister on several topics. But his inquisitive eyes were searching for the lost letter throughout the room. Soon his eyes stopped in a corner from where a letter was hanging on a rack beneath the mantle piece. Hitting upon a plan, he deliberately left his snuff-box on the table so that he can visit the Minister on the next day. And he did. And he did with perfect plan and preparation. He arranged for a chaos on the street by his own men at a certain hour. He entered the Minister's room within a few moments, a sound of a crying and shouting attracted them. Dupin reported the Minister that "a man with the musket" was firing frantically "among a crowd of women and children". So Dupin was able to distract the Minister's attention to the pandemonium on the street. In the meantime he became consciously busy in exchanging the purloined letter with a facsimile in which he wrote a line — Un dessin Si Funeste, S'il n'est digne d' Atree, est digne de Thyeste (a plot so hateful, if it is not worthy of Atreus, is worthy of Thyestes). This Line suggests that there were a brotherly enmity between Dupin and the Minister D —.

Once Minister D — severely offended Mr. Dupin in Vienna. He vowed to take revenge, waited for his good time; it came in the form of the Purloined Letter. He prepard to give lesson to the

Minister. And he did. The Minister, being unaware of the fact that he owns the letter no more, will try to play the trick upon the Queen to blackmail her, and thus will hasten his downfall. This is the game of intelligence Dupin played with the Minister. He studied the mind of the criminal and went one step ahead to defeat him. This method of observation of the criminal's psychology, playing with the criminals and defeating them in the mind game paved the way for popular detective stories. Mr. Dupin and the unnamed narrator became the model for the famous duo of English literature, Sherlock Holmes and Dr. Watson, written by Sir Arthur Conan Doyale. Both Dupin and Holmes were amature Sleuths, both were found of smoking pipe and their powerful weapon was the ability to probe into the psychological realm of the criminals and logical analysis and thereby infering the solutions. Both of them employ the theory of the ratiocination and they brilliantly use their intuitive intellect to solve any problem logically. Both Dupin and Holmes are originally eccentric in nature and they seem to be very private persons. Both of them had connection and acquaintances in many places. They prefer darkness specially in darkness of the evening which, they think, is very conducive for reflection. To solve a case, whatever complex it might be, they collect information and then ponder.

Over them deeply before any physical action. They are patient listeners, whenever any case arrives to them, they listen to it patiently; they love silence; and both of them are the expert in the human psychology of different nature. Not only that, they have immense knowledge on diverse topics of the universe.

On the other, Monsieur G— was the appropriate progenitor of the Scotland Yard Officers. The Police Prefect G— was sufficiently trained in his professional training but not well-skilled in imaginative intelligence. He had been assigned to investigate into the case of the royal epistle. He employed the force of Paris police as well as their professional knowledge. But he made a blunder at the beginning of his investigation; he underestimated the intelligence of the Minister D— on the ground that he writes poetry. Therefore Mr. G— infered that Minister D— was emotionally strong but intellectually weak. But he never thought that the Minister D— could be excessively clever. Mr. G— presumed that the letter must have been hidden in such a place that no one can find it. In absence of the Minister he searched his apartment inch by inch. It is a fact that Mr. G— had duplicate keys of all the apartments in the Paris. So he had no problem to carry out such investigation at whatever times he wishes. What he lacked was the knowledge of the criminal psychology and that lack of the knowledge led his whole endeavour to failure. That is why he visited Mr. Dupin who ultimately solved the problem and retrieved the purloined letter.

Some Literary Criticisms on The Purloined Letter

In 1844 Poe wrote to his friend, Mr James Lowell, "The Purloined Letter is perhaps the best of my tales of racioncination". In 1845 the story was published in a collection entitled *The Gift* and the editor opined that the story was "one of the aptest illustrations which could well be conceived of that curious play of two minds in one person".

However, such a novel story with novel technique courted literary criticisms from a number of critics specially in 1960s and 1970s. The famous theorist of the structuralist method Jacques Lacan opined that the content of the Queen's letter was irrelevant to the story and the proper place of the significance is determined by the symbolic structure in which its exists and is displaced. First by the Minister and then by Monsieur G—. In reply to Lacan's view, Jacques Derrida, the theorist of deconstruction method, pointed out what Lacan missed and suggested that it is not the letter which lacks meaning but Lacan himself made the lack of meaning. He also opined that the letter was a Castration of the King by the Queen, which Lacan is blind to. Barbara Johnson mediated the debate between Lacan's structuralist theory and Derrida's deconstructive theory and told that the letter belonged all long to the Queen as a substitute for a phallas.

Another critic Donald E. Pease commented that Lacan "equates the possession of a letter — defined as a 'lack' of content — with 'literal' as opposed to 'symbolic' castration, hence the odor of the feminine. On other words the 'possession' of the lack otherwise displaced by language identifies the possessor with the lack 'She' thinks she possesses. So femininity exists as an 'effect' of the delusion of possession of a lack otherwise displaced (as a masculine effect) by the endless purloining of the letter.'

And all these debates up to the mid 1980s are collected in an incomplete volume entitled *The Purloined Poe*. The work is incomplete in the sense that works like Richard Hull was not included.

ESSAYS ON THE PURLOINED LETTER

(a) Theme of the Purloined Letter

There is much novelty in the theme of **The Purloined Letter** in which Dupin figures out as the chief protagonist. The letter, of the Purloined Letter is the main theme of the story. C. Auguste Dupin has also remained as the protagonist in his two other stories The Murder in The Rue Morgue and The Mystery of Mary Roget. All these three stories of Poe set a new genre — the detective stories in which Mr. C. Auguste Dupin and the unnamed narrator appear in discussing the clue of mystery or the process of unlocking the problems. The letter, or the pruloined letter is the main theme of the story, The Purloined Letter. It is the source of power, source of money and the source of political control on political gain. And if we go thoroughly, we find that the letter is really the cause of a fuse of power.

The theme theory of The Purloined Letter may be termed as "Duality" which is the true nature of the humanity. That is the nature of the reality. This theme of duality is found best illustrated in Klenman Babenor's essay "The Shadow's Shadow: The motif of the Double in Edgar Allan Poe's The Purloined Letter" which appeared in the book *The Purloined Poe* edited by Muller and Richardson. In that essay Babenor writes:

"One aspect of the work offen noticed but as yet unexplained is the pervasive doubling motif that underlies the structure of the tale as whole and characterise particularly the relationship between M. Dupin and his rival the Minister D-. Poe's insistent use of doubling in the story considerably exceeds that which is necessary for presenting Dupin method of investigation, which in case stresses defection through psychological identification with an adversary. Rather the prominent pattern of doubles suggests that the protagonist and his foil are moral duplicates and may ultimately be two phases of the same mind".

Babener also opines that the double principle informs the basic action of the story, the major event of which Dupin's retrieval of the purloined letter and consequent triumph over the resourceful D—. The action revolves around Dupin's method of Investigation.

Another point of dualism is that the parallelisms and adjectives used to describe the major characters are compounded by an almost compulsory duplication of structural elements in story. Nearly every major movement of plot occurs twice. There are two meetings between the Prefect and Mr. Dupin. In the second visit of the Prefect the narrator describes that the Prefect "found was occupied very nearly as before". Both visits are at nights and both times the Prefect is supplied with pipe and chair. There were two interviews between Dupin and Minister D— as on each occasion they discuss the same topic. There are the searching by the police in Minister's apartment and the Minister's has been waylaid twice by police men in the streets in disguise of Thugs under the supervision of the Prefect. There are also two instances of blackmails — one by the Minister against the Queen and another by the Dupin against the Prefect to obtain payments for his help.

The chief theme of the story is, no doubt, the letter and its purloining and retrieving. One day a lady with royal dignity was reading a letter in her boudoir. The letter is secret one and probably from fiance. Suddenly her husband entered the room and the lady (Queen) put the letter on the table in a hurry. She could not keep it inside the drawer. In the meantime the Minister D — entered the room for an emergency work and he noticed the letter kept open the table. He identified the writer of the letter and sensing that an affair with the writer and the Queen, he estimated the high value of the letter. So, when he left the room, he took the letter of the Queen, leaving an unimportant letter in its place. The Queen was helpless and could not utter a word lest the affair would be disclosed to her husband who was standing near the elbow. Now the Minister was in a position to gain undue political advantages by blackmailing the Queen whose honour was in a great danger. So the Queen engaged the Prefect Mr. G — to retrieve the letter from the Minister. They waylaid the Minister twice in the disguise of Thug but the letter was not found. They searched the Minister's apartment at night when the Minister was not present in his home. They investigated all the chairs, tables, furniture, walls, floors, beds and every inch of all the rooms. They examined every possible corners with the powerful microscope. But all their ventures went in vain. The letter was found nowhere. So out of frustration and with a hope of getting some clues about the purloined letter, Mr. G — visited C. Auguste Dupin, the amateur private detective, who has already solved two complex cases; one in The Murder in the Rue Morgue another in The Mystery in Marie Roget. Monseur G — found Dupin in his room in Paris engaged in smoking pipe and discussing with his friend-cum-narrator. They were discussing about the adventures in The Murder in the Rue Morgue. The Prefect cut in their conversation and narrated his own problem, the purloined letter, Minister's attempts of blackmailing the queen for political gain, his attempts to retrieve the letter and his failure. Dupin listened to him patiently, asked a few questions, and advised that Paris police should search the house of the Minister again.

After a month the Prefect visits the detective again. He narrates his story of investigation with negative result. This time he adds that the Queen has declared 50,000 Francs for the letter. Dupin announces that if the Prefect gives him a check of 50,000 Francs, he will hand over the letter to him instantly. The Prefect became astonished; his facial expression proves that he could not believe his ears. In a tranced manner, he put the digits in a leaf of cheque book, passed it to the detective who is readily handed over the letter and without delaying a second, he almost ran out of the room in his tranced state to deliver the purloined letter to its real owner, the Queen.

Now it is Dupin's turn to explain to his narrator-friend how he succeeded in fetching back the valuable letter. Once the Minister offended him in Vienna. So he was determined to pay back his turn. He visited the minister's apartment in disguise weaning a pair of green glasses. He complained about his weak eyes. He was searching the room while talking with the Minister. He was found letters suspending from a mantle piece. He surveyed the outer envelope of the letter and intentionally left his gold snuff-box on the table of the Minister's room so that he could pay a second visit. The next day he visited again and after a few small talk, there was a pandemonium on the street near window of the Minister's apartment. Dupin informed the Minister that a man with a musket was firing at children and the women. The Minister tried to see through the window what was happening on the road and in the meantime, Dupin exchanged the letter with a facsimile which he prepared to befool the Minister. Inside the facsimile he inscribed: "Un dessin Si funeste, S'il n'est digne d'Atree, est digne de Thyeste" which mean "such a baneful scheme, if not worthy of Atreus, is worthy of Thyestes". Thus Dupin wanted to take his personal revenge by bringing about abrupt political downfall of the Minister D —.

So it is the dexterity of Poe to whom a petty, love letter could be a great theme of a detective story. And the mystery is quite simple because the person who purloined the letter is known. There is no murder or killing in the story; no bloodshed takes place ; only the game of wits and intelligence play vital to solve the mystery. Detective Dupin outwitted his opponent with his sharp wit and presence of mind. Here lies the success of the theme and Edgar Allan Poe is rightly called the father of the detective story.

(b) Appropriateness of the Title in The Purloined Letter

Ans. The title of The Purloined Letter says itself about the content of the story. From the title we can assume that the story is about a letter which is stolen or purloined. And when a letter is purloined, it must be remembered that it has immense value in it - whether political, social or something else. After going through the story we come to know that the letter contains some "message of affair". But we never know what that message is. We only know that it belonged to the royal lady—the Queen who lost the letter in the moment of 'accident'. Actually the letter was not stolen; it has been taken away cleverly by the Minister who wanted to enforce his political influence over the Queen. So the content of the letter is not important. The readers are only concerned with its effect of it. And it is obvious from the story that whoever possessor the letter, becomes psychologically powerful. So the letter act as a magic stick with which its possesses becomes mentally strong and confident. Such a letter must be a hot cake story which Poe presented in his The Purloined Letter.

C. Auguste Dupin and the narrator are joined by Prefect G -, the Chief of the Paris police. He narrates the theft of an important letter in few full view of its Royal recipient in presence of her husband.

The thief was none other than the powerful and crafty Minister D — who was in a position to defame the Queen and gain a political benefits at it was a letter about her affair. A healthy amount of reward was announced and the Paris police were engaged to recover the letter. The police under the leadership of the Prefect G—, took all possible measures to find it out, but no result came. The police had taken a part of all the furniture in the apartment of the Minister and thoroughly searched the adjacent houses. Dupin listened to the Prefect and advised him to reinvestigate the house of the Minister carefully again.

One month later, Mr. G— visits Mr. Dupin again in the same place in France. He reported of his failure and told that reward has been doubled to 50,000 Francs. Dupin told him to write the cheque of that amount and he promised to exchange the much wanted letter with Mr. G—.

Mr. G—became astonished, filled the cheque, gave it to Mr. Dupin who instantly handed him the Purloined letter. The man leaves the room almost panting.

Now, it is Dupin who explains how he has recovered the letter from the Minister's house. He tried to study the psychology of the Minister and accordingly he ran his investigation. He visited the Minister and eyed the letter in an open place, distressed and torn, in a letter rack below the mantle piece. He intentionally left his snuff-box on the table in the Minister's room so that he can visit the next day with his full preparation. He did so. A pre-arranged pandemonium was created on the road below the window of the

Minister's room to distract his attention. Dupin took the letter and replaced it with a dummy copy he had made earlier.

It is a fact that the word "purloined" would have disappeared from the Lexicon had Poe not used it in his famous detective story figuring Mr. Dupin. So in The Purloined Letter, not only the 'purloined' letter was recovered, but that mundane word becomes tre'schoulte. And to retrieve the letter, Dupin deduces nothing. He only used his simple observation, heavily tricked out, that the letter should be in simple place. And it is a matter of the study of human psychology. Some modern critics like Reising opined that it is Dupin who is in the clandestine lover of the Queen and who wrote that letter which was purloined. It is quite evident from his remarks to the narrator that the Minister D- "is well acquainted with my MS." Therefore, when he creates a facsimile of the letter, he does not sign on it with which he exchanges the Queen's billet-doux. Then the Minister would recognise his identity. So, those critics called Dupin a liar, and extortionist and humbug.

However, simply speaking, the purloined letter is like a mirror on which the reflection of all the characters, their inner-self and their psychology is seen clearly. The Queen is proved to be her husband, the King. The Minister is proved to be power hungry, cheat and a first hand criminal. He is cruel, crook and political eccentric. And he has a habit of intruding into other's affairs. The Prefect of Paris police proved his worthless professional skill devoid of imaginative power. And Mr. Dupin proved his psycho-analytic skill to measure the mind of a criminal. The mystery is solved by the Dupin and solved in manner, without bloodshed, without murder, without any violence.

Now a few questions remain unanswered in the story.

(i) If the letter was kept on a letter rack below the mantle piece, why did the police not find it; at least, have a look at it?

(ii) What type of benefit did the Minister want to gain—political or sexual? was he sexually attracted to the Queen?

(iii) What type of character was the King? Was he over simple or indifferent to his wife?

But in spite of all these shortcomings, the title The Purloined Letter exactly matches with its theme in the story The Porloined Letter.

(c) Narrative Technique in The Purloined Letter

The Purloined Letter is the third story of Dupin trilogy written by the Poe, the two other being The Murder in The Rue Morgue and The Mystery of Mary Roget. He crafted The Purloined Letter very meticulously, with seemingly sole attention to affecting the readers, not trying to make any kind of philosophical point. His work was not just topping into some interesting philosophical phenomenon, but the testament to what literary analysis actually should be. The techniques involved in the story make it so effective and popular. The Purloined Letter is narrated by an unnamed narrator who is Dupin's friend and roommate. This first person narrator does not take part in any of the major actions of the story. And the most unique to point to note is that The Purloined Letter opens with references to the action and experiences of The Murders in The Rue Morgue: the narrator thus I want to string the incidents between these two stories of the detective genre, though there is no murder, or bloodshed in The Purloined Letter.

The story begins with the long description of the "analytical mind" that delights in untangling a problem as an athlete enjoys physical exertion. The method he explains the truth is so perfectly analytical that it often seems like a natural instinct. He goes on to explain that though mathematics is similar to the art of analysis, it is not a pure calculation he is talking about. The superiority of a kind of emotional, sensitive, observational kind of intelligence is described here. The narrator is claiming that even in two games that are restricted to squares and pieces, the merely attentive player will only succeed to be a certain extent. Sensitive observation of human behaviour will become important at the story of progresses. The problem solving ability of Dupin has an analogy with a whist player who has a superior analytical brain which allow the player to win both the game and many problem of life. It is ability to observe beyond the game and to be creative that defines the Prefect. He has an intuition for all the physical and the emotional changes of the opposite player and therefore is able to tell what is a trick and what is genuine. In The Purloined Letter, Poe exaggerates this quality of analysis, making it seem like the most sought-after quality of intelligence-higher even than the flair of an ingemine. This is one of the methods Poe begins to play with our expectations. Dupin begins to reveal himself to be more than set of eccentric habits. He has the ability to see the narrator's thoughts, even though that appears to be steps removed from the scene at hand. This supernatural sense gives Dupin the upper hand and we see that the story revolves around his analytical sensitivity.

The description of Dupin's process of defecting the narrator's thoughts is long and complicated but Dupin doesn't seem to put any effort into it, it comes naturally to him. This gives him a special, intellectual power, Poe's stories often put a man of reason into a supernatural situation that overwhelms him. But Dupin seems to have a mind that combines reason and sensitivity in a way that can understand deeper mysteries, because it is itself mysterious. The way the narrator has introduced us to Dupin sets us up for a story about analysis and riddles. He has lulled us into a slow, methodical rhythm with his explanation of chess and whist.

By introducing the idea of an inept police force, Poe introduces the "thorough and well-reasoned" intellect, in contrast to Dupin's sensitive analysis. Such mundane thorough reasoning can do nothing in the face of the inexplicable. Dupin, however, who treats the whole thing like a game, seems more confident.

Poe effectively keeps the narrator in the dark just as we are being kept in the dark. As Dupin gradually, step by step, makes his case to the narrator, we are put in his shoes, and feel like we are in the midst of the situation. Dupin uses suspenses as if he is telling a story too, choosing to tell the narrator that the criminal is very clever and sinister in nature.

Critics often regard Poe as a father of detective stories and in this story he employs crime solving technique which emphasises or thinking like the criminals. C. Auguste Dupin's theory of solving crimes involves an act of thinking like target people i.e. criminals. The Detective enters into the realm of the psychology of the criminal and tries to feel "thought pulse" of the criminal. This theory is called psycho-analysis which Dupin employes for his opponent to solve the mystery and set an example for his posterior generation like Sherlock Holmes, Poirot or Feluda.

(d) Art of Characterisation in the Purloined Letter

Ans: Edgar Allan Poe exposed mastery of art of characterisation in his popular short story The Purloined Letter. His characters belong to the higher social status, above from common social level. Some are from Royal blood, some are politically powerful and some are intellectually superior than other. They indulge scandalous affairs, plotting and intriguing. They have the uncanny nature of making a mountain from a molehill.

Now, let us examine all the characters in the story.

QUEEN: The royal lady, according to some critics, is from the French royal family. But another group of critics hold that she is a fictitious character. Whatever else, she is the victim of corrupt political force. But it is also true that she herself is corrupt, deceitful, irresponsible and impressively powerful. She is engaged in a scandalous affair about which the Royal King is not aware of it. She deceits her husband with a letter of her fiancé in her hand and she wished to cancel the letter from the Royal man. The letter is 'openly' stolen and the thief is known to her. She secretly employs the Police force to retrieve the letter. Otherwise her royal honour was in question to cover up the illegitimate affair. She even didn't hesitate to expend money that rightfully belonged to people of France. And the power thus attained has, for months part, been wielded for political purposes to a very dangerous extent. Simply speaking, what she's doing might be bad for people of France.

MINISTER D —: The character of the Minister D- is very complex one who has affinity towards the poetry as well as the mathematics. He is equally well in the composition of a poem or solving the problem of a differential calculus. He is an official villain who holds tremendous, political power. He is the strongest political opponent of the Queen. He cunningly steal a letter from the Queen's apartment and use it to blackmail her to achieve his political benefits. The Minister is not only cunning but psychologically intelligent who keeps the letter in an open place in such a manner that the police cannot trace it. However, the letter is finally retrieved by Minister's friend and his ideological, psychological antagonist, Mr. Dupin, the detective.

MR. DUPIN: C. Auguste Dupin is the detective in the story. The Purloined Letter also appeared in the story The Murder of Rue Morgue, the first story of the detective genre developed by Poe. He has a creative mind, observant nature and analytical spirit. When the Paris police failed to trace the letter, he used the psychological power and stayed one step ahead of the criminal i.e. the Minister. He holds that the Paris police were using these in original methods that they learnt in the professional training. To solve the problem in The Purloined Letter, he reveals the capacity for revenge. He did not forget insult made by the Minister in the Vienna years before. His mode of investigation thrives on intuition and individual cunning. The character of C. Auguste Dupin is rather a foil to the character of Minister D—.

THE POLICE PREFECT: Monsieur G —, the police Prefect is the political ally of the Queen. He is in charge of finding the missing letter he employ all his police force as well as his searching methods to retrieve the letter that may protect the Queen's honour. But he is too methodical and mechanical in his work. Although he is smart enough. He approaches to Mr. Dupin for assistance and he informs the reward for the letter that the Queen announce on it returning. The Prefect here does a two-fold duty - recovering the letter and recovering the secret affair of the Queen who is under threat of her scandalous affair to be public. He is very loyal to the loyal lady otherwise we would not trust upon him. Like the Queen, Mr. G - is also crooked and corrupt who keeps all the duplicate keys that can open any chamber or cabinet in Paris. Not only that, it seems to us that he co-operates the Queen for the money, declared secretly in the form of prize. He is undoubted by a corrupt player in a corrupt system.

Other minor characters in the story are the royal king and the narrator both of whom are nameless. The royal king, the husband of the royal lady, is lied and deceived. He has no influence either on the Queen or on the Minister D-. Both deceive him equally. The Queen put the letter in front of him without letting him know the content of the letter. Edgar Allah Poe mentioned him as “a third person”, “the third personage”’ and “the other exalted personage”. He was really a powerless King.

Another minor character is the narrator who is intimate friend of Dupin. He is the close associate of the Dupin in his Paris residence. He narrates the story but does not take part directly in any major action of the story. Although nameless, he is the most important character in the story. He shapes the story with a clear bias towards Dupin as we found Dr. Watson biasness towards Sherlock stories.

(e) Solution of Mystery vs. Mystery of Solution: Element of the Suspense in The Purloined Letter

Ans. The Purloined Letter is the only story of Edgar Allan Poe’s three ‘tales of raciocination’ in which the “mystery” does not involve murder. In The Purloined Letter, there is a backdrop of ‘affair of count” of a high-level political intrigue and struggles over a power involving a female “royal personage” another “exalted personage” and a “power hungry Minister”. The matter is as the police Prefect Mr. G — put it, “that a certain document of the last importance, has been purloined from the royal apartments. The individual who purloined it is known; It is known, also, that it still remains in his possession” and the situation is “becoming of more and more important everyday”.

Jacques Lacan puts it in the following way: “We shall find illumination in what at first was seems to obscure matters: the fact that the tale leaves us in virtually total ignorance of the sender no less than of the contents of the letter. We are told only that the Minister immediately recognised the handwriting of the address and only incidentally, in a discussion of the Minister Camouflagé, is it said that the original seal fore the ducal arm of the S family. As for the letters beaning, we know only the danger it entails should it to come into the hands of a specific third party, and that its possession has allowed the Minister to “wield, to a very dangerous extent, for political purposes”, the power assures him over the interested party.

But all this tells us nothing of the message it conveys. Love letter or conspirational letter, letter of betrayal or letter of mission, letter of summons or letter of distress, we are assured of but one thing: the Queen was not to bring it to the knowledge of the lord and master.

Rather the Queen engaged Mr. G—, the Parisian police Prefect to find out the letter. The Prefect investigates every nook and corner of the premises of the Minister. This is the painstaking but a doomed exercise. The Minister had been twice waylaid, as if G—, foot pads, and disguised police person searched the Minister rigorously under Mr. G -'s supervision but with zero outcome.

The Prefect who disliked/ underestimated poet and poetry, guided his mission of searching the letter with a Mathematical conception. He conceived of space as empty, three-dimensional, and isotropic, and objects in that space and rigid figure. The Prefect's mind was totally filled with Euclidean geometry governed by congruence. The Prefect looked for the letter that remains the same object, independent of its position. He searches for a space that could contain the object by dividing up the Minister; furniture and apartment into the series of compartments. But being disappointed by all his labourious methods that resulted in a negative, the police Prefect approached to Mr. Dupin, the detective who helped him to solve the mystery in The Murder in The Rue Morgue.

Now it is Dupin's turn to show his magic of ratiocination. He is always engaged in mental reflection. Dupin's repeated allusions to Mathematics in speaking of "analysis" serves as Poe's reminder that the term has various technical mathematical meanings. In The Purloined Letter, the methods of analysis are brought to bear on a mystery that revolves around problem of space. The Prefect cannot find the letter because he has a rigid, limited notion of the letter and the space where the minister has hidden it; Dupin for his part recognises the letter immediately and hides his theft of it by conceptualizing the principal at play in the Minister's ploy. Dupin's solution represents a synthesis of these produces — a resolution to the same mystery is Mathematics: how to reconcile analytic and Geometric approach to problem of space.

Dupin exchanged the original letter with that of the facsimile inside which the following lines were inscribed:

— Un dessin Si funeste,

Sil r'est digne d'Atree, est digne de Thyste.

They are to be found in Gefillon's "Atrace".

There are the mysterious lines of personal revenge; they are translated as follows —

" A design so deadly,

If not worthy of Atreus,

Is worthy of Thystes".

In the art of solving the mystery of the purloined letter, the detective Dupin takes his personal revenge against the Minister. The fact is that the Minister was acquainted with Dupin and there was an enmity between them. That enmity, undoubtedly added some spice to the mystery of The Purloined Letter.

(f) Theme of Power and Politics

The study of The Purloined Letter is the study of power, politics and corruption. All the major characters in the story are engaged in the game of power and politics and the letter is the pivotal object that plays a vital role as a controlling force of power. Movement of the letter from hand to hand shift the centre of power. It also highlights the diminutive forces of royal families the face of a corrupted Minister's order.

When the theft occurred in the Queen's chamber, King was there standing beside the Queen. But he referred to as the "third person" whom neither the Queen nor the Minister gave importance to. The Queen cheated him by putting the letter that was very personal to her in such a manner that the King had no interest to look at it. But the Minister found it on the table and within seconds he understood the handwriting and measured the importance of the letter. Ignoring his majesty's presence, the Minister slyly exchanged the letter with that of an unimportant one. Hence both the Queen and the Minister ignored the King's presence and it shows the degradation of Royal power.

Now it becomes a psychological tussle between the Queen and the Minister and the latter wants to take an upper hand or the former. He is in a position to blackmail the Queen and thus enjoy the free hand to use or misuse his political power. Honour of the royal family was at stake. The Minister must have a fond intention in his mind that the letter would give him a certain power in the certain quarters where such power is immensely valuable. So the letter becomes a symbol of a power struggle and a point of preserving honour of an elite family of French society. Minister D- was so power hungry and desperate that anyhow he wanted to have "ascendancy over the illustrious personage whose honour and peace was so jeopardised."

The power thus attained by the Minister has, for some months past, been wielded, for political purposes, to a very dangerous extent. In the words of the Prefect, "the personage robbed is more thoroughly convinced everyday, of the necessity of reclaiming her letter. But this, of course cannot be done openly. In fine, driven to despair, she has her committed the matter to me".

So the police Prefect, Monsieur G— , takes over the charge of retrieving the valuable personal letter. And for that purpose he used the "power" which he enjoys as police Prefect of Paris as well as close associate of the Queen. He searched the Minister's hotel during his absence and without his least knowledge that such an investigation is going on in his hotel. The police took notice that the Minister remains frequently absent from the home all night. His servants sleep at the night at a distant place and most of them remain drunk at night. The Prefect has duplicate keys of the Minister's home. For three months a night has not passed, during the greater part of which the Prefect is engaged himself in ransacking the Minister's hotels. Obviously prestige of Paris police was related there. But more than that, the great secret was the enormous reward which was declared by the Queen. But whatever the Prefect did, he did it without result and so he appeared before the detective Dupin if he can give any idea to solve the mystery.

As soon as the detective heard the story of The Purloined Letter, he hit upon his own plan of politics to tackle the Minister who once harassed him in Venice. He promised a good revenge and the moment has come to last.

He argues: When I wish to find out how wise, or how stupid, or how good, or how wicked, is anyone, or what are his thoughts at the moment, I fashion the expression of him, and then wait to see what thoughts or sentiments arise in my mind or heart, as if to match or correspond with the expression." He deeply studied the psychology of the Minister who, according to him, is a Mathematician and a poet. He quoted from Chamfort to describe the nature of the Minister: "que toute idee publique, toute convention recure, est une Sottise, car elle a convenn an plus grand mombre" (It is safe to wage that every public idea and every accepted convention is sheer foolishness, because it has suited the majority). So he adopted the strategy of an eight year boy whose success at guessing in the game of 'even or odd' marbles depended on "an identification of the reasoner's intellect with that of his opponent." Dupin was resolute to beat the minister on his own turf.

So he did. He visited the Minister's house in disguise. He found the letter hanging from a mantle-piece. He again played a game of politics by diventing the Minister's attention towards the roadside and in the meantime exchanging the letter of the Queen with a facsimile prepared by himself with a note inside;

"Un dessin Si funeste Sil n'est digne d'Atree, est digne de Thyeste".

Thus, the game of the revenge is complete. Now he feels the power of the letter. The Prefect pays a second visit to Dupin and by the by he says that the prize has been increased up to a double amount as compared to its primary amount. He also said casually that he himself will give a check for fifty thousand Francs to one who can give him the letter. Dupin told him to write the cheque and sign it. When the Prefect with full astonishment did so, Dupin handed him the original letter which he was hunting for like an eagle. From now on, whenever the Minister will try to blackmail the Queen, he will undoubtedly count his own political downfall. That is a sweet revenge of Mr. Dupin.

(g) Theory of Game Clue to Solve the Riddle

It is no exaggeration that Edgar Allan Poe is the undisputed father of American Short Story. He gave a birth to a totally new genre of American literature hidden to unknown, 'that affords unmentionably the fairest field for the exercise of the loftiest talent'. It is true that

Poe did not have a ready-made device called the short fiction in his time, but after Poe a distinctive kind of writing had already permanently inscribed itself onto the American literature world.

Poe composed three short stories of a detective genre, which is better described as the 'tales of ratiocination' and they are:

(a) The Murder in The Rue Morgue;
(b) The Mystery of Marie Roget; and
(c) The Purloined Letter.

The first two stories are full with murders, bloodshed and they are grotesque and arabesque in nature. But the third one is the tale of ratiocination without blood or murder but "a parable of act of analysis" (Irwin). The Purloined Letter is a reason for solving the mystery. It is a work with more gratuitions and more generous meditation on the problems at hand. The tale of an ratiocination gives a Canny mind at work, whose meditation and explanation over a Purloined letter becomes a good work of literature topping of an ending genre which would come to be coupled with the fate of the American literature.

The central character in The Purloined Letter is, of course Mr. Dupin, the amateure detective of Paris, who lives with his partner who is the narrator of all heroic activities of Dupin. Mr. Dupin is the detective whose chief weapon is his brain. He is fond of smoking Meer schaum and broods over things specially in darkness. One such evening in Paris, Mr. G–, the Parisian police Prefect met Mr. Dupin and informed about a missing letter that belonged to the Queen of France and the letter was Purloined Openly from the Chamber of the royal lady. It was secret letter probably from the fiancé of the Queen and the thief who took it was none other than the influential and crooked Minister D —.The Prefect engaged his police force as well as his searching methods to bring the letter back but in vain. He employed all his technical and professional knowledge but found no trace of the letter. He searched all the furniture of the Minister's home during his absence at night. He examined every inch of the room, its walls, floors and even the legs of the chairs and tables. But there was no sign of the letter. He even waylaid the Minister on the way so that he might carry the letter with him, but without result. At last, the Prefect came to Mr Dupin to seek his help and advice. C. Auguste Dupin is a man of constant mental reflection. He began to study the psychology of his opponent who must be a cunning rogue. Dupin cites the story of a school boy of eight years of age, whose success at guessing in the game of "even and odd" attracted universal applaud. The game is very simple and is played with marbles. One player holds in his hand a number of marbles and the opposition has to guess whether the number of the marbles is "even or odd". If the guess is correct, the guesser gets one marble. But in the case of wrong he loses one. The boy of Dupin's story won all the marbles of the school. He has some principle of guessing which includes observation and admeasurement of the astuteness of his opponent. Dupin in this way explains the method of wining: "For example, a Simpleton is his opponent, and, holding up his closed hand, asks, "even or odd" our school boy replies, "odd", and loses; but upon the second trial he wins, for he then says to himself, "the Simpleton had them even upon the first trial, and his amount of cunning is just sufficient to make him have them odd upon the second: I will therefore guess odd; "— he guesses odd, and wins." This is the method of the school boy who win every time over his opponents with his analysis, an identification of the reason's intellect with that of his opponent.

And this is the game of intellect with which C. Auguste Dupin won the prize at last. The Prefect underestimates the Minister's intellect as he was an Mathematician. But Dupin contracted with this idea and argued that the Mathematical reason has long been regarded as the reason par excellence. So he analysed the psychology of the Minister in the way the school boy became successful in retrieving the purloined letter.

(h) Critics on The Purloined Letter

Ans: (1) Nathaniel Hawthorne (Twice - Told Tales, May 1842):

"But it is of his tales that we desire principally to speak. The tales proper, in our opinion, affords unquestionably the fairest field for the exercise of the loftiest talent, which can be afforded by the wide domains of mere prose.... A skillful literary artist has constructed a tale. If wise, he has not fashioned his thoughts to accommodate his incidents; but having conceived, with deliberate care, a certain unique or single effect to be wrought out, he then invent such an incidents — he then combines such events as may best aid him in establishing this preconceived effect. If his very initial sentence tend not to the outbringing of this effect, then he has failed in his first step. In the whole composition there should be no word written, of which the tendency, direct or indirect, is not to the one pre-established design. And by such means, with such care and skill, a picture is at length painted which leaves in the mind of him who can contemplate it a kindred art, a sense of the fullest satisfaction. The idea of the tale has been presented unblemished, because undisturbed; and this is an end unattainable by the novel.

Arthur Conan Doyle: (Matthews)

"... in his carelessly prodigal fashion, threw out the seeds from which so many of our present forms of literature have sprung, [he] was the father of the detective tale, and covered it limits so completely that I fail to see how his followers can find any fresh ground which they can confidently call their own. For the secret of the thinness and also of the intensity of the detective story is, that the writer is left with only one quality, that of intellectual acuteness, with which to endow his hero. Everything else is outside the picture and weakens the effect. The problem and its solution must form the theme, and the character-drawing be limited and subordinate. On this narrow path the writer must work, and he sees the foot marks of Poe always in front of him. He is happy if he ever finds the means of breaking away and striking out some little side track of his own".

Barabara Johnson: The fame of Reference: Poe, Lacan, Derrida

(i) "It is act of analysis which occupy the centre of the discursive stage, and the act of analysis of the which is some way disrupts that centrality. In the resulting asymmetrical, abssal structure, no analysis—including this one—can intervene without transforming and repeating other elements in the sequence, but which nevertheless produces certain regular effects". (110)

(ii) "The problem of psychoanalytical triangularity... is not that it contain the wrong number of terms, but that it presupposes the possibility of the successful dialectical mediation and harmoniums normalization, or Aufhebung, of desire. The three terms in the Oedipal triad enter into a opposition whose resolution resembles the synthetic moment of a Hegelian dialectic. (122)

Jacques Lacan: Seminar on The Purloined Letter

"The primal scene is thus of performed, we are told, in the royal boudoir, so that we suspect that the person of the highest rank, called the exalted personage", who is alone there when she receives a letter, is the Queen. This feeling is confirmed by the embarrassment into which she is plunged by the entry of the other "exalted personage", of whom we are already been told prior to this account the knowledge he might have of the letter in the question would jeopardize for the lady, nothing less than her honour and safety...

Dupin calls on the Minister. The letter receives him with studied non-challance, affecting in his conversation romantic ennui. Meanwhile Dupin, whom this pretence does not deceive, his eyes protected by green glasses, proceeds to inspect the premises. When his glance catches a rather crumpled piece of paper apparently thrust carelessly into a division of an ugly Paste board and rack, hanging gaudily from the middle of the mantle piece — he already knows that he's found what he's looking for. His conviction is reinforced by the very details which seem to contradict the description he has of the stolen letter, with the exception of the format, which remains the same.

5. Jacques Derrida: The Purvery or of Truth

"The issue involved could be evaluated by the way of any number of different standards. Within the cultural boundaries of my personal reference and because of analysis begun elsewhere, I believe that collaboration of this problematic must at the present time pause for the consideration of Jacques Lacan's proposed reading of Freud, or, more specifically, within the space of this article, "Seminar on The Purloined Letter".

Those "literary critics" in France who have not yet posed of the question of the text. Their interest as well as their fecundity lay elsewhere. It seems that the same applies equally and without injustice to Marie Bonaparte's psycho-biography, any psychoanalysis of material imagination, existential psychoanalysis, psycho-criticism, a thematic phenomenology colored by psychoanalysis etc".

2

The Crack-Up

F. Scott Fitzgerald (1896-1940)

Francis Scott Fitzgerald was born in St. Paul, Minnesota, U.S.A. on 24 September, 1896. He was Christened as Francis Scott Key Fitzgerald, in honour of his second cousin Mr. Francis Scott Key, who was the composer of the National Anthem of the U.S.A. His father Edward was a businessman with least financial success and his mother Molly McQuillan was an Irish lady. Born in an upper middle class family and living in the fashionable residential neighbourhood of Sumit Avenue, the Fitzgerald family earned distasteful comments from critics who called them "a certain genteel shabbiness". Due to insufficient monetary condition. Fitzgerald dropped out of Princeton University to join the U.S. army. *This Side of Paradise* was his first novel published in 1920 and Fitzgerald became the ideal of spokesman of the decade which is fondly only called as jazz age.

Fitzgerald was married to Zelda, a beautiful and sober lady from South and moved to Paris for a life of art, culture and literature. His second novel *The Beautiful and the Damned* was published in 1922 and it is achieved least success. But his third novel, *The Great Gatsby* was a masterpiece that tells the story of a gangster who deliberately pursuit for rich girl but remained unsuccessful. But happiness was but a mirage in Fitzgerald's life. He became too much alcoholic and his wife Zelda became a psychiatric patient. Amongst the great depression of Thirties, Fitzgerald published his another successful novel *Tender Is The Night* in 1934. The title of this novel has been taken from Keats' famous poem *Ode To Nightingale* and it tells about a psychiatrist who is destroyed by his wealthy wife.

He could not complete his final novel *The Last Tycoon* which is about a complex movie produced life story. Fitzgerald published four collections of short stories including 164 stories with popular success. This versatile author, novelist, essayist, screenplay writer and short story writer died at the age of 44 on 21 December, 1940 in Hollywood, U.S.A.

An Introduction to the Story

Fitzgerald wrote three essays with a view to clearly establish profoundly different groups of people in American society. His group instead of delineating different needs share the same set of values are those curtailed by those who are most powerful. The readers are able to comprehend the Sham consciousness of America, depicting the restlessness, mental derangement and pretentiousness of the society.

A society within and without to life, without a stake in the fond business, without a girl, without order in the world and without conviction, Lional Trilling describes in the following way:

"The power of the love in Fitzgerald, then, went hand in hand with a sense of personal responsibility and perhaps erected it. But it happens that the tragic hero can conceive and realise a love that is beyond his own prudence or beyond his powers of dominance or self-protection, so that he is destroyed by the very thing that gives him his spiritual status and structure".

The Crack Up was published in 1936. It is the collection of three essays namely 'The Crack Up', 'Pasting It Together', and 'Handle With Care', which are commonly called the trilogy of depression.

These essays are autobiographical in nature and he describes his own experience of depression and alcoholism. He also narrates his wife Zelda's bipolar psychiatric disorder through metaphorical terms. These essays are rather Fitzgerald's beauty confessions of his own life.

The Crack-Up

F. Scott Fitzgerald

Part I

Of course all life is a process of breaking down, but the blows that do the dramatic side of the work — the big sudden blows that come, or seem to come, from outside — the ones you remember and blame things on and, in moments of weakness, tell your friends about, don't show their effect all at once. There is another sort of blow that comes from within — that you don't feel until it's too late to do anything about it, until you realize with finality that in some regard you will never be as good a man again. The first sort of breakage seems to happen quick — the second kind happens almost without your knowing it but is realized suddenly indeed.

Before I go on with this short history, let me make a general observation — the test of a first-rate intelligence is the ability to hold two opposed ideas in the mind at the same time, and still retain the ability to function. One should, for example, be able to see that things are hopeless and yet be determined to make them otherwise. This philosophy fitted on to my early adult life, when I saw the improbable, the implausible, often the "impossible," come true. Life was something you dominated if you were any good. Life yielded easily to intelligence and effort, or to what proportion could be mustered of both. It seemed a romantic business to be a successful literary man — you were not ever going to be as famous as a movie star but what note you had was probably longer-lived; you were never going to have the power of a man of strong political or religious convictions but you were certainly more independent. Of course within the practice of your trade you were forever unsatisfied – but I, for one, would not have chosen any other.

As the Twenties passed, with my own twenties marching a little ahead of them, my two juvenile regrets — at not being big enough (or good enough) to play football in college, and at not getting overseas during the war — resolved themselves into childish waking dreams of imaginary heroism that were good enough to go to sleep on in restless nights. The big problems of life seemed to solve themselves, and if the business of fixing them was difficult, it made one too tired to think of more general problems.

Life, ten years ago, was largely a personal matter. I must hold in balance the sense of futility of effort and the sense of the necessity to struggle; the conviction of the inevitability of failure and still the determination to "succeed" and, more than these, the contradiction between the dead hand of the past and the high intentions of the future. If I could do this through the common ills — domestic, professional, and personal — then the ego would continue as an arrow shot from nothingness to nothingness with such force that only gravity would bring it to earth at last.

For seventeen years, with a year of deliberate loafing and resting out in the center — things went on like that, with a new chore only a nice prospect for the next day. I was living hard, too, but: "Up to forty-nine it'll be all right," I said. "I can count on that. For a man who's lived as I have, that's all you could ask."

—And then, ten years this side of forty-nine, I suddenly realized I had prematurely cracked.

Now a man can crack in many ways — can crack in the head, in which case the power of decision is taken from you by others; or in the body, when one can but submit to the white hospital world; or in the nerves. William Seabrook in an unsympathetic book tells, with some pride and a movie ending, of how he became a public charge. What led to his alcoholism, or was bound up with it, was a collapse of his nervous system. Though the present writer was not so entangled — having at the time not tasted so much as a glass of beer for six months — it was his nervous reflexes that were giving way — too much anger and too many tears.

Moreover, to go back to my thesis that life has a varying offensive, the realization of having cracked was not simultaneous with a blow, but with a reprieve.

Not long before, I had sat in the office of a great doctor and listened to a grave sentence. With what, in retrospect, seems some equanimity, I had gone on about my affairs in the city where I was then living, not caring much, not thinking how much had been left undone, or what would become of this and that responsibility, like people do in books; I was well insured and anyhow I had been only a mediocre caretaker of most of the things left in my hands, even of my talent.

But I had, a strong sudden instinct that I must be alone. I didn't want to see any people at all. I had seen so many people all my life — I was an average mixer, but more than average in a tendency to identify myself, my ideas, my destiny, with those of all classes that came in contact with. I was always saving or being saved — in a single morning I would go through the emotions ascribable to Wellington at Waterloo. I lived in a world of inscrutable hostiles and inalienable friends and supporters.

But now I wanted to be absolutely alone and to arrange a certain insulation from ordinary cares.

It was not an unhappy time. I went away and there were fewer people. I found I was good-and-tried. I could lie around and was glad to, sleeping or dozing something twenty hours a day and in the interval trying resolutely not to think — instead I made lists — made lists and tore them up, hundreds of lists: of cavalry leaders and football players and cities, and popular tunes and pitchers, and happy times, and hobbies and houses lived in and how many suits since I left the army and how many pairs of shoes (I didn't count the suit I bought in Sorrento that shrank, nor the pumps and dress shirt and collar that I carried around for years and never wore, because the pumps got damp and grainy and the shirt and collar got yellow and starch-rotted). And lists of women I'd liked, and of the times I had let myself be snubbed by people who had not been my betters in character or ability.

— And then suddenly, surprisingly, I got better.

— And cracked like an old plate as soon as I heard the news.

That is the real end of this story. What was to be done about it will have to rest in what used to be called the "womb of time."[11] Suffice to say that after about an hour of solitary pillow-hugging began to realize that for two years my life had been a drawing on resources that I did not possess, that I had been mortgaging myself physically and spiritually up to the hilt. What was the small gift of life given back in comparison to that? — when there had once been a pride of direction and a confidence in enduring independence.

I realized that in those two years, in order to preserve something

— an inner hush maybe, maybe not — I had weaned myself from all the things I used to love — that every act of life from the morning toothbrush to the friend at dinner had become an effort. I saw that for a long time I had not liked people and things, but only followed the rickety old pretence of liking. I saw that even my love for those closest to inc had become only an attempt to love, that my casual relations — with an editor, a tobacco seller, the child of a friend, were only what remembered I should do, from other days. All in the same month I became bitter about such things as the sound of the radio, the advertisements in the magazines, the screech of tracks, the dead silence of the country — contemptuous at human softness, immediately (if secretively) quarrelsome toward hardness — hating the night when I couldn't sleep and hating the day because it went toward night. I slept on the heart side now because I knew that the sooner I could tire that out, even a little, the sooner would come that blessed hour of nightmare which, like, a catharsis, would enable me to better meet the new day.

There were certain spots, certain faces I could look at. Like most midwesterners, I have never had any but the vaguest race prejudices — I always had a secret yen for the lovely Scandinavian blondes who sat on porches in St. Paul but hadn't emerged enough economically to be part of what was then society. They were too nice to be "chickens" and too quickly off the farmlands to seize a place in the sun, but I remember going round blocks to catch a single glimpse of shining hair — the bright shock of a girl I'd never know. This is urban, unpopular talk. It strays afield from the fact that in these latter days I couldn't stand the sight of Celts, English, Politicians, Strangers, Virginians, Negroes (light or dark), Hunting People, or retail clerks, and middlemen in general, all writers (I avoided writers carefully because they can perpetuate trouble as no one else can) — and all the classes as classes and most of them as members of their class;...

Trying to cling to something, I liked doctors and girl children up to the age of about thirteen and well-brought-up boy children from about eight years old on. I could have peace and happiness with these few categories of people. I forgot to add that I liked old men — men over seventy, sometimes over sixty if their faces looked seasoned'. I liked Katherine Hepburn's face on the screen, no matter what was said about her pretentiousness, and Miriam Hopkins's face, and old friends if I only saw them once a year and could remember their ghosts.

All rather inhuman and undernourished, isn't it? Well, that, children, is the true sign of cracking up.

It is not a pretty picture. Inevitably it was carted here and there within its frame and exposed to various critics. One of them can only be described as a person whose life makes other people's lives seem like death — even this time when she was cast in the unusually unappealing role of Job's comforter. In spite of the fact that this story is over, let me append our conversation as a sort of postscript:

"Instead of being so sorry for yourself, listen —" she said. (She always says "Listen," because she thinks while she talks — really thinks.) So she said: "Listen. Suppose this wasn't a crack in you — suppose it was a crack in the Grand Canyon."

"The crack's in me," I said heroically.

"Listen! The world only exists in your eyes — your conception of it. You can make it as big or as small as you want to. And you're trying to be a little puny individual. By God, if I ever cracked, I'd try to make the world crack with me. Listen! The world only exists through your apprehension of it, and so it's much better to say that it's not you that's cracked — it's the Grand Canyon."

"Baby, et up all her Spinoza?"

"I don't know anything about Spinoza. I know —" She spoke, then, of old woes of her own, that seemed, in telling, to have been more dolorous than mine, and how she had met them, overridden them, beaten them.

I felt a certain reaction to what she said, but I am a slow-thinking man, and it occurred to me simultaneously that of all natural forces, vitality is the incommunicable one. In days when juice came into one as an article without duty, one tried to distribute it — but always without success; to further mix metaphors, vitality never "takes." You have it or you haven't it, like health or brown eyes or honor or a baritone voice. I might have asked some of it from her, neatly wrapped and ready for home cooking and digestion, but I could never have got it — not if I'd waited around for a thousand hours with the tin cup of self-pity. I could walk from her door, holding myself very carefully like cracked crockery, and go away into the world of bitterness, where I was making a home with such materials as are found there — and quote to myself after I left her door:

"Ye are the salt of the earth. But if the salt hath lost its savour, wherewith shall it be salted?"

Matthew 5:13"

Part II

In a previous article this writer told about his realization that what he had before him was not the dish that he had ordered for his forties. In fact — since he and the dish were one, he described himself as a cracked plate, the kind that one wonders whether it is worth preserving. Your editor thought that the article suggested too many aspects without regarding them closely, and probably many readers felt the same way — and there are always those to whom all self-revelation is contemptible, unless it ends with a noble thanks to the gods for the Unconquerable Soul.

But I had been thanking the gods too long, and thanking them for nothing. I wanted to put a lament in my record, without even the background of the Euganean Hills to give it color. There weren't any Euganean Hills that I could see.

Sometimes, though, the cracked plate has to be retained in the pantry, has to be kept in service as a household necessity. It can never again be warmed on the stove nor shuffled with the other plates in the dishpan; it will not be brought out for company, but it will do to hold crackers late at night or to go into the icebox under leftovers.

Hence this sequel — a cracked plate's further history.

Now the standard cure for one who is sunk is to consider those in actual destitution or physical suffering — this is an all-weather beatitude for gloom in general and fairly salutary daytime advice for everyone. But at three o'clock in the morning, a forgotten package has the same tragic importance as a death sentence, and the cure doesn't work — and in a real dark night of the soul it is always three o'clock in the morning, day after day. At that hour the tendency is to refuse to face things as long as possible by retiring into an infantile dream — but one is continually startled out of this by various contacts with the world. One meets these occasions as quickly and carelessly as possible and retires once more back into the dream, hoping that things will adjust themselves by some great material or spiritual bonanza. But as the withdrawal persists there is less and less chance of the bonanza — one is not waiting for the fade-out of a single sorrow, but rather being an unwilling witness of an execution, the disintegration of one's own personality.

Unless madness or drugs or drink come into it, this phase comes to a dead end, eventually, and is succeeded by a vacuous quiet. In this you can try to estimate what has been sheared away and what is left. Only when this quiet came to me did I realize that I had gone through two parallel experiences.

The first time was twenty years ago, when I left Princeton in junior year with a complaint diagnosed as malaria. It transpired, through an X-ray taken a dozen years later, that it had been tuberculosis — a mild case, and after a few months of rest I went back to college. But I had lost certain offices, the chief one was the presidency of the Triangle Club, a musical comedy idea, and also I dropped back a class. To me college would never be the same. There were to be no badges of pride, no medals, after all. It seemed on one March afternoon that I had lost every single thing I wanted — and that night was the first time that I hunted down the specter of womanhood that, for a little while, makes everything else seem unimportant.

Years later I realized that my failure as a big shot in college was all right — instead of serving on committees, I took a beating on English poetry, when I got the idea of what it was all about, I set about learning how to write. On Shaw's principle that "if you don't get what you like, you better like what you get," it was a lucky break — at the moment it was a harsh and bitter business to know that my career as a leader of men was over.

Since that day I have not been able to fire a bad servant, and I am astonished and impressed by people who can. Some old desire for personal dominance was broken and gone. Life around me was a solemn dream, and I lived on the letters I wrote to a girl in another city. A man does not recover from such jolts — he becomes a different person, and, eventually, the new person finds new things to care about.

The other episode parallel to my current situation took place after the war, when I had again overextended my flank. It was one of those tragic loves doomed for lack of money, and one day the girl closed it out on the basis of common sense. During a long summer of despair I wrote a novel instead of letters, so it came out all right, but it came out all right for a different reason. The man with the jingle of money in his pocket who married the girl a year later would always cherish an abiding distrust, an animosity, toward the leisure class – not the conviction of a revolutionist but the smoldering hatred of a peasant. In the years since then I have never been able to stop wondering where my friends money came from, nor to stop thinking that at one time a sort of droit du seigneur might have been exercised to give one of them my girl.

For sixteen years I lived pretty much as this latter person, distrusting the rich, yet working for money with which to share their mobility and the grace that some of them brought into their lives. During this time I had plenty of the usual horses shot from under me – I remember some of their names —Punctured Pride, Thwarted Expectation, Faithless, Show-off, Hard Hit, Never Again. And after a while I wasn't twenty-five, then not even thirty-five, and nothing was quite as good. But in all these years I don't remember a moment of discouragement. I saw honest men through moods of suicidal gloom — some of them gave up and died; others adjusted themselves and went on to a larger success than mine; but my morale never sank below the level of self-disgust when I had put on some unsightly personal show. Trouble has no necessary connection with discouragement — discouragement has a germ of its own, as different from trouble as arthritis is different from a stiff joint.

When a new sky cut off the sun last spring, I didn't at first relate it to what had happened fifteen or twenty years ago. Only gradually did a certain family resemblance come through — an overextension of flit flank, a burning of the candle at both ends; a call upon physical resources that I did not command, like a man overdrawing at his bank. In its impact this blow was more violent than the other two but it was the same in kind — a feeling that I was standing at twilight on a deserted range, with an empty rifle in my hands and the targets down. No problem set — simply a silence with only the sound of my own breathing.

In this silence there was a vast irresponsibility toward every obligation, a deflation of all my values. A passionate belief in order, a disregard of motives or consequences in favor or guesswork and prophecy, a feeling that craft and industry would have a place in any world — one by one, these and other convictions were swept away. I saw that the novel, which at my maturity was the strongest and supplest medium for conveying thought and emotion from one human being to another, was becoming subordinated to a mechanical and communal art that, whether in the hands of Hollywood merchants or Russian idealists, was capable of reflecting only the tritest thought, the most obvious emotion. It was an art in which words were subordinate to images, where personality was worn down to the inevitable low gear of collaboration. As long past as 1930, I had a hunch that the talkies would make even the best selling novelist as archaic as silent pictures. People still read, if only Professor Canby's book of the month — curious children nosed at the slime of Mr. Tiffany Thayer in the drugstore libraries — but mere was a rankling indignity, that to me had become almost an obsession, in seeing the power of the written word subordinated to another power, a more glittering, a grosser power....

I set that down as an example of what haunted me during the long night — this was something I could neither accept nor struggle against, something which tended to make my efforts obsolescent, as the chain stores have crippled the small merchant, an exterior force, unbeatable — (I have the sense of lecturing now, looking at a watch on the desk before me and seeing how many more minutes —).

Well when I had reached this period of silence, I was forced into a measure that no one ever adopts voluntarily: I was impelled to think it God, was it difficult! The moving about of great secret trunks. In the first exhausted halt, I wondered whether I had ever thought. After a long time I came to these conclusions, just as I write them here:

(1) That I had done very little thinking, save within the problems of my craft. For twenty years a certain man had been my intellectual conscience. That was Edmund Wilson.

(2) That another man represented my sense of the good life, though I saw him once in a decade, and since then he might have been hung. He is in the fur business in the Northwest and wouldn't like his name set down here. But in difficult situations I have tried to think what he would have thought, how he would have acted.

(3) That a third contemporary had been an artistic conscience to me — I had not imitated his infectious style, because my own style, such as it is, was formed before he published anything, but there was an awful pull toward him when I was on a spot.

(4) That a fourth man had come to dictate my relations with other people when these relations were successful: how to do. What to My." How to make people at least momentarily happy (in opposition to Mrs Post's theories of how to make everyone thoroughly uncomfortable with a sort of systemized vulgarity).' This always confused me and made me want to go out and get drunk, but this man had seen the game, analyzed it, and beaten it, and his word was good enough for me.

(5) That my political conscience had scarcely existed for ten years save as an element of irony in my stuff. When I became again concerned with the system I should function under, it was a man much younger than myself who brought it to me, with a mixture of passion and fresh air.

So there was not an "I" anymore — not a basis on which I could organize my self-respect — save my limitless capacity for toil that it seemed I possessed no more. It was strange to have no self — to be like a little boy left along in a big house, who knew that now he could do anything he wanted to do, but found that there was nothing that he wanted to do —

(The watch is past the hour and I have barely reached my thesis. I have some doubts as to whether this is of general interest, but if anyone wants more, there is plenty left, and your editor will tell me. If you've had enough, say so — but not too loud, because I have the feeling that someone, I'm not sure who, is sound asleep — someone who could have helped me to keep my shop open. It wasn't Lenin, and it wasn't God.)

Part III

I have spoken in these pages of how an exceptionally optimistic young man experienced a crack-up of all values, a crack-up that he scarcely knew of until long after it occurred. I told of the succeeding period of desolation and of the necessity of going on, but without the benefit of Henley's familiar heroics, "my head is bloody but unbowed." For a checkup of my spiritual liabilities indicated that I had no particular head to be bowed or unbowed. Once I had a heart but that was about all I was sure of.

This was at least a starting place out of the morass in which I floundered: "I felt—therefore I was." At one time or another there had been many people who had leaned on me, come to me in difficulties or written me from afar, believed implicitly in my advice and my attitude toward life. The dullest platitude monger or the most unscrupulous Rasputin who can influence the destinies of many people must have some individuality, so the question became one of finding why and where I had changed, where was the leak through which, unknown to myself, my enthusiasm and my vitality had been steadily and prematurely trickling away.

One harassed and despairing night I packed a briefcase and went off a thousand miles to think it over. I took a dollar room in a drab little town where I knew no one and sunk all the money I had with me in a stock of potted meat, crackers, and apples. But don't let me suggest that the change from a rather overstuffed world to a comparative asceticism was any Research Magnificent — I only wanted absolute quiet to think out why I had developed a sad attitude towards sadness, a melancholy attitude toward melancholy, and a tragic attitude toward tragedy — why I had become identified with the objects of my horror or compassion.

Does this seem a fine distraction? It isn't: identification such as this spells the death of accomplishment. It is something like this that keeps sane people from working. Lenin did not willingly endure the sufferings of his proletariat, nor Washington of his troops, nor Dickens of his London poor. And when Tolstoy tried some such merging of himself with the objects of his attention, it was a fake and a failure. I mention these because they are the men best known to us all.

It was dangerous mist. When Wordsworth decided that "there hath passed away & glory from the earth," he felt no compulsion to pass away with it, and the Fiery Particle Keats never ceased his struggle against T.B. nor in his last moments relinquished his hope of being among the English poets.

My self-immolation was something sodden-dark. It was very distinctly not modern - yet I saw it in others, saw it in dozen men of honor and industry since the war. (I heard you, but that's too easy- there were Marxians among these men.) I had stood by while one famous contemporary of mine played with the idea of the Big Out for half a year; I had watched when another, equally eminent, spent months in an asylum unable to endure any contact with his fellowmen. And of those who had given up and passed on I could list a score.

This led inc to the idea that the ones who had survived had made some sort of clean break. This is a big word and is no parallel to a jailbreak when one is probably headed for a new jail or will be forced back to the old one. The famous "Escape" or "Run away from it all" is an excursion in a trap even if the trap includes the South Seas, which are only for those who want to paint them or sail them. A clean break is something you cannot come back from; that is irretrievable because it makes the past cease to exist. So, since I could no longer fulfill tire obligations that life had set for me or that I had set for myself, why not slay the empty shell who had been posturing at it for four years? I must continue to be a writer because that was my only way of life, but I would cease any attempts to be a person — to be kind, just, or generous. There were plenty of counterfeit coins around that would pass instead of these and I knew where I could get them at a nickel on the dollar. In thirty-nine years an observant eye has learned to detect where the milk is watered and the sugar is sanded, the rhinestone passed for diamond and the stucco for stone. There was to be no more giving of myself— all giving was to be outlawed henceforth under a new name, and that name was Waste.

The decision made me rather exuberant, like anything that is both real and new. As a sort of beginning there was a whole shaft of letters to be tipped into the wastebasket when I went home, letters that wanted something for nothing — to read this man's manuscript, market this man's poem, speak free on the radio, indite notes of introduction, give this interview, help with the plot of this play, with this domestic situation, perform this act of thoughtfulness or charity.

The conjurer's hat was empty. To draw things out of it had long been a sort of sleight of hand, and now, to change the metaphor, I was off the dispensing end of the relief roll forever.

The heady villainous feeling continued.

I felt like the beady-eyed men I used to see on the commuting train from Great Neck fifteen years back — men who didn't care whether the world tumbled into chaos tomorrow if it spared their houses.45 He was one with them now,— one with the smooth articles who said:

"I'm sorry but business is business."

Or:

"You ought to have thought of that before you got into this trouble.

Or:

"I'm not the person to see about that."

And a smile —- ah, I would get me a smile. I'm still working on that smile. It is to combine the best qualities of a hotel manager, an experienced old social weasel, a headmaster on visitors' day, a colored elevator man, a pansy pulling a profile, a producer getting stuff at half its market value, a trained nurse coming on a new job, a body-vender in her first rotogravure, a hopeful extra swept near the camera, a ballet dancer with an infected toe, and of course the great beam of loving kindness common to all those from Washington to Beverly Hills who must exist by virtue of the contorted pan.

The voice too — I am working with a teacher on the voice. When I have perfected it the larynx will show no ring of conviction except the conviction of the person I am talking to. Since it will be largely called upon for the elicitation of the word "Yes," my teacher (a lawyer) and I are concentrating on that, but in extra hours. I am learning to bring into it that polite acerbity that makes people feel that far from being welcome they are not even tolerated and are under continual and scathing analysis at every moment. These times will of course not coincide with the smile. This will be reserved exclusively for those from whom I have nothing to gain, old worn-out people or young struggling people. They won't mind – what the hell, they get it most of the time anyhow.

But enough. It is not a matter of levity. If you are young and you should write asking to see me and learn how to be a somber literary man writing pieces upon the state of emotional exhaustion that often overtakes writers in their prime – if you should be so young and fatuous as to do this, I would not do so much as acknowledge your letter, unless you were related to someone very rich and important indeed. And if you were dying of starvation outside my window, I would go out quickly and give you the smile and the voice (if no longer the hand) and stick around till somebody raised a nickel to phone for the ambulance, that is if I thought there would be any copy in it for me.

I have now at last become a writer only. The man I had persistently tried to be became such a burden that I have "cut him loose" with as little compunction as a Negro lady cuts loose a rival on Saturday night. Let the good people function as such - let the overworked doctors die in harness, with one week's "vacation" a year that they can devote to straightening out their family affairs, and let the underworked doctors scramble for cases at one dollar a throw; let the soldiers be killed and enter immediately into the Valhalla of their profession. That is their contract with the gods. A writer need have no such ideals unless he makes them for himself, and this one has quit. The old dream of being an entire man in the Goethe-Byron-Shaw tradition, with an opulent American touch, a sort of combination of J.P. Morgan, Topham Beauclerk, and St. Francis of Assisi, has been relegated to the junk heap of the shoulder pads word for one day on the Princeton freshman football field and the overseas cap never worn overseas.

So what? This is what I think now: that the natural slate of the sentient adult is a qualified unhappiness. I think also that in an adult the desire to be finer in grain that you are, "a constant striving" (as those people say who gain their bread by saying it) only adds to this unhappiness in the end — that end that comes to our youth and hope. My own happiness in the past often approached such an ecstasy that I could not share it even with the person dearest to me but had to walk it away in quiet streets and lanes with only fragments of it to distill into little lines in books — and I think that my happiness, or talent for self-delusion or what you will, was an exception. It was not the natural thing but the unnatural — unnatural as the Boom; and my recent experience parallels the wave of despair that swept the nation when the Boom was over.

I shall manage to live with the new dispensation, though it has taken some months to be certain of the fact. And just as the laughing stoicism which has enabled the American Negro to endure the intolerable conditions of his existence has cost him his sense of the truth — so in my case there is a price to pay. I do not any longer like the postman, nor the grocer, nor the editor, nor the cousin's husband, and he in turn will come to dislike me, so that life will never be very pleasant again, and the sign Cave Canem is hung permanently just above my door. I will try to be a correct animal though, and if you throw me a bone with enough meat on it I may even lick your hand.

Word notes and Annotations

PART I

Blows — Turbulence; Shock; Hard stroke with hand or weapon.
Finality — Closing, Conclusive
Breakage — Broken thing; breaking
Improbrable — Difficult to believe; absurd
Implausible — Doubtful; dubious
Juvenile regrets — Teenage repentant
War — War is here referred to the first world war (1914 - 1918).

Resolved themselves into a childish waking dreams of imaginary heroism.

1920s was Jazz age in America. It was an age of miracles, art, excess and also an age of Satire. This period was called "roaring Twenties" when America became a powerful nation.

Then the ego would continue as an arrow Shot from nothingness to nothingness—

Here 'ego' refers to self-revelation of oneself. Emphasis is given here to a preoccupation with the past and to make a meaningful in the context with the present in one's life.

Suddenly realized I had prematurely cracked — Age and ambitions always go parallel and they never meet together. And this Faustian contract is found in almost all Fitzgerald fictions. Fitzgerald believed that age cannot be a sentimental guarantor of wisdom.

William Seabrook — William Buchlor Seabrook (1884 - 1945) was an American writer and traveller. He was the author of the book 'Asylum' which was published in 1933 and it became the best seller in the USA incidentally Seabrook himself was and a patient in a mental institution for the treatment of alcoholism.

Wellington at Waterloo — Duke of Wellington, Field Marshal Arthur Wellesley (1769 - 1852) was a British soldier and statesman. He defeated the army of Napolean Bonaparte in 1815 at the war of Waterloo.

Inscrutable — Mysterious; Impenetrable

Dozing — Sleeping lightly

Cavalry — Soldiers who fight on horse back or vehicles.

Sorrento — A small, beautiful Italian city with sea cliffs.

Snubbled — Humiliated

Weaned — Accustomed

Screech — Harsh scream

Yen — Intense desire or longing

Blondes — light-cloured, fair haired girls.

Faces looked Seasoned — Faces marked with lines and marks that prove the old age.

Katherine Hepburn — Katherine Houghton Hepburn (1907-2003) was an American actress on stage and screen. She was a popular actress with box-office success.

Miriam Hopkins — Ellen Miriam Hopkins (1902 - 1972) was an American actress. She starred in Trouble in Paradise which brought her fame and acclaim.

Job's comforter — Job is a biblical character who faced enormous disaster and his friends pretended to comfort him but in reality they tried to find fault with him.

The Grand Canyon — It is a great Canyon carved by the Colorado river. This is situated in the state of Arizona of the U.S.A.

Spinoza — Baruch Spinoza (1632-1677) was a Dutch philosopher. He composed "Ethios Demonstrated in Gometrical order?

"Ye are the Salt of the earth. But if the Salt hath lost its savour, wherewith shall it be Salted" — This Gospel exists in the New Testament. This is the story of Jesus who being driven out of Israel, went up into a mountain and preached to his disciples.

PART II

Editor — Arnold Gingrich, the editor of Esquire magazine.

Euganean Hills — P.B. Shelley's (1792 - 1822) poem 'Lines written Among the Enganean Hills' is referred to here. These group of hills are situated in the north of Italy.

Shuffled — Mixed up or rearranged

Beautitude — Blessedness

Bonanza — Source of great wealth

Flank — side of body between ribs and hip.

Jingle — clinking noise

Animosity — Hostility

Smoldering — Burning with flame

Droit du Seigneur — Supposed right of a feudal lord to have sexual relations with a vassal's bride on her wedding night.

Deflation — Reduction of money to combat inflation.

Collaboration — Co-operation

Archaic — Of early period or old.

Professor Canby — Professor Henry Seidel Canby (1878-1916) was a professor at Yale University. He was the founder editor of the "Saturday Review of Literature'.

Tiffany Ellworth Thayer (1902-59) — Tiffany Ellworth Thayer was an American Actor and novelist. His best selling novel was 'Thirteen Women' published in 1930.

Rankling — Causing persistent annoyance

Indignity — Insult

Obsolescent — Waning

Edmund Wilson — Edmund Wilson (1895-1972) was an American anthor and critic.

That another man — Ernest Miller Hemingway (1899-1961), the famous American author is mentioned here.

That a fourth man — Here the reference goes to Gerald Murphy (1888-1964) with whom Fitzgerald met in France in 1924.

Lenin — Vladimir Ilyicn Lenin (1870-1924) was a Russian Communist revolutionary leader, statesman and writer. He became the prime minister of the Soviet Union in 1922.

PART III

Desolation — Abandonment

Henley — Willian Ernest Henley (1849-1903) was an English poet. His famous poem was 'Invictus'.

Morass — Entanglement

Floundered — Struggle helplessly

Platitude — Commonplace remark

Rasputin — Grigori Efimovich Rasputin (1872-1916) was peasant monk of Siberia. He was the religious advisor of Nicholas II. Later he was assassinated by Russian noblemen.

Asceticism — Self-discipline

Proletariat — Working class

Washington — George Washington (1732-1799) was a famous American military leader. He led the Revolutionary war of America from 1775 to 1783. He became the first President of America.

Dickens — Charles Dickens (1812-1870) was the famous English novelist. His popular novels are 'David Copperfield', 'Bleak House' etc.

Tolstoy — Leo Tolstoy (1828-1910) was the Russian philosopher and author. His two great novels are 'War and Peace' and 'Anna Karenina'.

Wordsworth — William wordsworth (1770 -1850) is the great English Romantic poet. The line quoted here is taken from his famous peom "Ode: Intimation of Immortality from Recollections of Early Childhood."

Keats — John Keats (1795 - 1821) is one of the greatest later Romantic poets. He died of T.B. in the early age of 22.

Self-immolation — Self-sacrifice

Sodden-dark — Saturated darkness

Marxians — Followers of Karl Marx

Asylum — Shelter; Sanctuary

Irretrievable — That cannot be restored

Counterfeit — Imitation

Stucco — Plaster or cement for coating walls.

Indite — put into words; write

Sleight — Dexterity in conjuring

Great Neck — Great Neck is a place situated in the state of New York.

Weasel — Flesh eating mammal

Rotogravure — Type or process of printing

Compunction — Guilty feeling

Goethe-Byron-Shaw — Goethe was a German novelist and dramatist; Byron was a British Romantic poet; George Bernard Shaw was a modern Irish-English dramatist and critic.

J.P. Morgan — John Pierpont Morgan was a famous American Banker.

Tophan Beaeucherk — Tophan Beeuclerk was a famous 18th century wit who was friend to Dr. Johnson and Havace Walpole.

St. Francis of Assissi — He was an Italian monk who founded the Francisian order of friars.

Boom — Boom refers to the euphoria of 1920s of America.

Cave Cavem — (Latin phrase) Beware the dog.

Critical Summary of the Crack-Up

The Crack-Up is a collection of essays, previously unpublished letters and notes and it was published in 1945. It is the story of a psychiatrist who weds one of his patients. While she slowly recovers, the husband exhausts his vitality until he is " Un homme epuise" i.e. 'a man is used up'. However, the essay is in a three-part:

(i) The Crack-Up
(ii) Pasting it Together and
(iii) Handle with Care.

Part I: Crack-Up

In the beginning of the essay Fitzgerald asserts his readers that there are two kinds of blows a person face in his life. The first kind of blow has its impact very quick and immediate. The second type of blow has a very slow impact which, when detected, is too late to mend. Then the author went on an autobiographical way to describe his youth when all the problems of life were easy to deal with. But as years progressed. Fitzgerald found it difficult to tackle those problems and ultimately it was found that he was cracked-up.

In the state of crazy mood, the author could not stand anything or anyone except the image of Katherine Hepburn on-screen, children and doctors. At the end of the essay the author describes an interview with an critic who tried to boost the confidence of the author with her lively Spirits. But it has no effect on the author. His life became bitter and he was tending towards a gloomy world. He ended the first part with a quote from Mathew 5:15 "ye are the salt of the earth. But if the salt Hath lost its savour, wherewith shall it be salted?" (You are the salt of the earth. But if the salt has lost its taste, with which it be salted?"

Part II : Pasting It Together

The title of the second essay in the series is Pasting It Together. The self-revealation of the author enriched this part and his self revealation never end up in a positive tone. Here the author cites the reasons why he faces such tremendous breakdown. Owing to illness, he has to loss one valuable year in Princeton University. He has to leave the offices like the Triangle Club and other offices. He also faced a disastrous love affair that ended in naught due to lack of money. His personal defeats seemed to mingle with the national plight of changing the old world order replaced by a newer one. His novels that was transformed into films got very little success.

All those bitter experiences of life led him to be cracked up. The author felt that due to his dependent nature on several people for aesthetic, or intellectual purpose, he lost his self-identity. So he expressed his strong belief at the end of the essay that he is eager to search for his self-identity and individual existence which one existed in his character.

Part III: Handle with Care

The third essay of the series is entitled as "Handle with Care". It narrates the consequences of 'Crack up' moments of life of the author. The author felt it deeply that if he wants to survive, he must have to take a 'clean break'. He wanted to be an author and he tried to lose his identity as a person. He wanted to be a 'writer only' who cares for nothing except his own profits. He groomed his voice and smile to make a new personality of his own. The author finished the essay with a sarcastic but realistic comment wins on materialistic view of life. He says, "I will try to be a correct animal though, and if you throw me a bone with enough meat on it I may even lick your hand".

Critical Commentary on the Crack-Up

The Crack-Up series contains three essays written by Fitzgerald. These essays are basically self-revealing and the tone is often nostalgic. These pieces are rather the evidence of the author's stunted emotional growth and his perpetual adolescence. He is, indeed, a great writer and his greatness lies in his use of metaphors and smiles. An examples of a rich simile in his extended comparison of the broken writer to a cracked plate. Fitzgerald had an uncanny habit of looking backward rather than forward through his writing as evident in his "Echoes of the Jajj Age" published in 1931. In this essay he expressed his nostalgic feelings for the 1920's. He candidly admits that some readers will detect in his "pre-mature astereoschlerosis". In "My Lost City" Fitzgerald mourns for the past which is never retrievable. He reminisces the white and glittering city of New York in his memory.

Only the first essay of the series is titled as 'The Crack up' but gradually it became the umbrella title of the series of essays. In these essays Fitzgerald unlocked his personal emotions such as Zelda's mental condition, from which she never recovered. Fitzgerald himself became ill and dispirited. He had to live a life of mean standard in a cheap hotel in Hendersinville, North Carolina. All these incidents of the life are reflected in the present essay-series "The Crack-Up".

In an atmosphere of gloom and depression, Fitzgerald could not continue writing as he did earlier. This state of psychological depression led him to compose the essay series "The Crack Up". In the first essay in title "The Crack Up" Fitzgerald narrates about two kinds of blows that an individual faces in the life. Those blows can destroy the personality of an individual. One blow comes from outside and another blow is generated within the internal state of mind which is difficult to identify. To describe the 'blows" in his own life, Fitzgerald described his past life, say, at the age of twenty when he had lots of dreams and life seemed to him is an easy going manner. He began his career as a writer and life was going smoothly for a period only. Then he faced odd and difficult situations that hindered his progress and he needed to struggle to survive and succeed. Fitzgerald was hoping against hope that things will be alright for him and he will resume his life again in the proper way. But everything went against his plan and he 'cracked' prematurely, resulting "too much anger and too many tears".

In his essay we can have realistic pictures of the roaring twenties and gloomy thirties. The depression was the social stigma that left a sudden change in American Society and it is the Great Depression of 1929.

But whatever the condition, may be, life cannot remain stand still. Fitzerald tried to soothe his mind and tried to find out "certain insulation from ordinary cares" that comes from day to day's life. It was astonishing fact when he alienated from the rest of the society, he feel better to some extent. He became aware about "the sound of radio, the advertisements in the magazines, the screech of tracks", Fitzerald could manage to look at the picture of Katherine Hepburn on the screen with his old friends once in a years.

During the end of 1920s, Fitzgerald's physical health also began to deteriorate beside his psychological health. He felt a sense of insecurity and loneliness. At this point, his wife's condition was also getting worse with these financial crisis and mental breakdown, it became totally impossible for him to continue his profession as a writer. And, according to Donaldson, Fitzgerald could not "infuse his fiction with the emotional power he had once commended".

All the essays of the "Crack-Up" series describe Fitzgerald's personal gloomy state of mind as well as problems of the changing world of the thirties. In the first essay he talked about the sudden crack up of the author's nerves. In the face of gloomy and pessimistic situation, Fitzgerald could not compose contents with positive and optimistic tone. A modern author like Fitzgerald echoed the pessimistic view of the contemporary modern American society that characterises the alienation, futility and a sense of defeat.

In the second essay Fitzgerald tried to give an account of the nature of the blow that he received and its effect on his personal life. The immediate effect was that he lost the "Princeton's Triangle Club" and a few other offices resulting in his inability of winning medals for his college. There was another blow in his life and it was more fatal. He had a love affair and this affair ended it in a futile result due to the lack of money. It was an undoubtedly a severe blow in the author's mind. Gradually he lost his confidence and the sense of failure and discouragement haunted his life incessantly.

The third essay entitled the "Handle with Care" is an endeavor to recover from anxiety and deep depression. It is an essay with social sarcasm written in a satiric tone that makes an attempt to highlight the contemporary society with the selfish and materialist people. Fitzgerald is giving here a survival strategy, i.e. his decision to take a break from miserable life. At the end of this essay Fitzgerald sarcastically narrates that he has become a 'non person' author who, if given a bone enough meet on it, is ready to lick the hands of those benevolent persons. He beautifully narrated the contrasting features of the booming 1920s and the depression 1930s.

ESSAYS ON "THE CRACK - UP"

(a) Title of "The Crack - Up"

F. Scott Fitzgerald's *The Crack-Up* was published serially in a Esquire magazine in 1936 and in 1945 it was published in the book form with uncollected pieces, note books and letters written by Fitzgerald and edited by Edmund Wilson. The Crack up series contains three essay entitled 'The Crack Up', 'Pasting It Together' and 'Handle with Care' and all these essays confession of Fitzgerald's personal life and they document his spiritual and physical determination in the period of turmoil in mid thirties.

In one place of the essay 'the crack up', Fitzgerald wrote, "If I could do this through the common ills — domestic, professional and personal — then the ego would continue as an arrow shot, from nothingness to nothingness with such force that only gravity would bring it to earth at last". Here the self-revealation of the author has a cathasfic effect and a preoccupation with the past to make a sense of the present. Sigmund Freud's psychoanalysis was no longer a matter of theoretical topic, but the Clark University of the U.S.A. (Masachussetts) introduced psycho-analysis in their school's curriculum. Freud himself confessed: " As I stepped onto the platform, it seemed like the realisation of some incredible daydream: psychoanalysis was no longer a product of delusion — it has become a valuable part of reality". Psychoanalysis and its allied fields, its way of looking at things and self—had trickled in simplified forms, into the popular American literary works of 1930s and we find a self-defeating Faustian contract in almost all the fiction of Fitzgerald. Age is not a sentimental guarantor of resolution in his characterizations, even not in The Crack Up series of essays.

As for example, in the novel of Fitzgerald "The Great Gatsby", Daisy's husband Tom Buchaman is introduced as having "been one of the most powerful ends that ever played football at New Haven — a national figure in a way, one of those men who reach such an acute limited excellence at twenty one that evening afterward savors anti-climax. In "Tender Is The Night" when Dick Diver meets Rosemary Hoyt after a gap of long four years, it seems that their relationship as well as his worth is in transaction:

"The past drifted back and he wanted to hold her eloquent giving-of-herself in its precious shell, till he enclosed it, till it no longer existed outside him. He tried to collect all that might attract here it was less than it had been four years ago. Eighteen might look at thirty four through a rising mist of adolescence; but twenty-two would see thirty-eight with discerning clarity. Moreover, Dick had been at an emotional pick at the time of the previous encounter. Since then there had been a lesion of enthusiasm".

Once Fitzgerald defined his Crack-Up essay as "Trilogy of Depression" which not only highlight the psychological breakdown of the person but also their reaction towards "the spiritual change of life — and most unwilling one". The Crack-Up essays of Fitzgerald were written and published in 1930s and these are the reflection of his own life; to say the truth, Crack-Up essays are the confessions of the author in an autobiographical tone.

But it will make an in-depth study of those essays, it can be deciphered that they are not just personal pangs and depression of an individual, rather they reflect the contemporary social picture of America that witnessed a depression social condition after the boom of 1920s.

In the first essay that bears the leading title as "The Crack-Up", testifies the individual experience of the author that he has prematurely cracked up in life. He has become lonely and alienated from amongst the other fellows in the society. He could only tolerate a few things like Kathe Hepburn's image on the screen, children of a particular age and only doctors. His life was going to be intolerable, indeed. In the second entitled "Pasting It Together" Fitzgerald gives reasons why he faced such a breakdown in life. He had some blows in flows in life that might have changed the course of his life. The first blow was that he had some illness and owing to this illness he had to stop visiting the Triangle Club as well as Princeton University. He lost a year in the University and it ultimately left a negative impression in his life. The second blow was that he had to be separated from his loved one due to lack of money and this incident how a tragic effect in his life. All these incidents had impact on the mind of Fitzgerald and eventually he cracked up. In the third essay "Handle with Care", Fitzgerald gives an account of the effects or consequences that he had undergone during the crack up moment. He realized that he needs a break from his mundane activities. There is a sarcastic stone throughout this essay and to materialise his ambition, he is even ready to lick someone's hand if someone throws him a bone with enough meat on it.

To conclude, it may be said that the title of the essay "The Crack-Up" is appreciate.

Once Fitzgerald wrote to the American literary editor Maxwell Perkins in 1937, "You are about only friend who does not see fit to incorporate or moral lesson, especially since the Crack-Up stuff". The Crack up essays courted serene criticism also especially by Earnest Hemingway in his "The Snows of Kilimanjaro" published in the *Esquire* in 1936. He said that Scott Fitzgerald has been wrecked by his worship of the rich. And if not completely, Hemingway is true to some extent.

(b) The Jazz Age Versus The Great Depression

Ans: The Jazz Age refers to certain period between 1920 and 1930 when Jazz music and the dance styles rapidly gained popularity throughout the nation in the U.S.A. It is the cross-culture conjunction with the Roaring Twenties that gives little importance to prohibition Erar. Jazz music was the music of the younger generation and 1920s is called the "golden age" of Jazz music. Jazz music was fast, heavily syncopated and sometimes made up on the spot through improvisation. And also credit goes to F. Scott Fitzgerald who coined the term "The Jazz Age" to describe anything that goes flamboyant that characterises the 1920s.

There is controversy regarding who was the first man to start the Jazz music in America. According to some critic, it was Buddy Bolden who started the first jazz band in the U.S.A. in 1895. Another group of critics hold that in 1917, Nick Larocca and his original dixieland Jazz Band recorded the first Jazz music..." Livery Stable Blues". Jazz is a music genre originated by the Afro-American communities in New Orleans in the U.S.A. and its chief characteristics are swing and blue notes, call and response vocals, polyrhythms and of course, improvisation.

The American literary movement was influenced greatly by the Jazz age that defined American art, culture and literature. The Jazz tradition taught people to ask questions the ideas that they had about what was appropriate, normal and to be desired. If "The Crack-Up" is called the "autobiography as history", another essays by Fitzgerald entitled "Echoes of the Jazz Age" may be called the "history as biography" which is nothing but the reading lens of the previous one. He composed his essay in 1931, two years after the great depression of 1929, when the Wall Street stock market faced a devastating crash and there was an economic hardship, unemployment, distress, migration, acute food shortage and homelessness in the country. Fitzgerald reminisces about the roaring twenties and in the face of utter hopelessness of the great depression, he tells about the blind optimism of the coming future. His way of narrating the essay is like the telling the biography of a person. An excerpt from "Echoes From The Jazz Age" will testify that biography mingles with the history:

"The Jazz age had a wild youth and a heady middle age. There was the phase of the necking parties, the Leopold-Loef murder (I remember the time my wife was arrested on Queens Borough Bridge on the suspicion of being the 'bob-haired Bandit') and the John held clothes. In the second phase such a phenomena as sex and murder became more mature, if much more conventional.

Middle age must be serred and pajamas came to the beach to save fat thighs and flabby calves from competition with the one piece bathing-suit. Finally skirts came down and everything was concealed.... It was borrowed time anyhow — the whole upper tenth of a nation living with the insouciance of grand dukes and the casualness of chorus girls".

The thirties was an anthropomorphised decade and the great depression was a frightening senescence of it. President John Calvin Coolidge in his final state of the Union Address in 1929, said, "No Congress ... ever assembled has met with a more pleasing prospect then that which appears at the present time. ... in the domestic field there is tranquility and contentment ... and the highest record of prosperity in years". This was, no doubt, a false optimism in the face of tremendous financial depression. The Crack-Up essay bear the testimony of all these false hopes and deadening despair with the vocabulary of the 1920s finance markets, their optimistic growth and the state politics also is an emotive stone.

The Crack-Up stories, which are the autobiography of F.S. Fitzgerald, affected the American writers of the early mid twentieth century for their affinity towards Freudian genre. In the Crack-Up the psychoanalysis of the author is clear in almost every line of the text : "... a man can crack in many ways, can crack in the heads, in which case the power of decision is taken from you by others — or in the body, when one can but submit to the white hospital world — or in the nerves". Fitzgerald's The Crack UP is the science of psycho-analysis which is merged with the art of survey. It is the personal diary of Fitzgerald who also narrates the social effect of the Great Depression. It is the autobiography of an cracked up by individuals written in the Crack-Up time living in a cracked up society.

(c) Self-Revealation of Fitzgerald in 'The Crack-UP'

F. Scott Fitzgerald's The Crack-Up essays are the works of self-revealation and the self-confession. The Crack-Up consist of three essay namely, The Crack-Up, Pasting It Together and The Handle with Care were published in 1936 in *Esquire* consecutively in February, March and April issues. This self-revealation in literary writing created a new genre in American literature and this genre was imbibed by the next generations of American writers like Franklyn, Andubon, Thoreau and Whitman. This trend of self-expression or self-revealation in literature was successfully continued by the poets and writers of the sixties such as Lowell, Berryman and Sylvia Plath. Fitzgerald is the pioneer was who was able to analyse his past experience under the light of the present writing context.

In 1951, Fitzgerald's biography *The Far Side of Paradise* by the author Mizener was published and the darker elements of Fitzgerald's life in later years begin to expose to the readers and critics of Fitzgerald, too, began to reassess his works beside his success. James Miller opined that "Crack-Up" essays are embarrassing because Fitzgerald is obviously still keenly involved in a losing emotional struggles to become cuned". Not only the author, but almost all heroes of Fitzgerald try to hold onto an impossible hope. The Great Gatsby, the doomed hero Jay Gatsby "talked a lot about the past and I gathered that he wanted to recover something, some ideas of himself perhaps, that had gone into a loving Daisy. His life had been confused and disordered. Since then, but if he could once return to a certain starting place and go over it all slowly, he could find out what that thing was ... and once there is he could such on the pap of life, gulp down that incompatible milk of wonder". (Morris)

Here is an excerpt from "The Crack-Up" which testifies that The Crack-Up is surely self-revealation.

"Life, ten years ago, was largely a personal matter. I must hold in balance the sense of necessity to struggle; the conviction of the inevitability of failure and still the determination to "succeed" — and, more than these, the contradiction between the dead hand of the past and high intentions of the future. If I could do this through the common ills — domestic, professional and personal — then the ego would continue as an arrow shot, from nothingness to nothingness with such force that only gravity would bring it to earth at last". Here the 'ego' refers to "infantile dream" which is an acute emphasis on self-revealation on catholic, or preoccupation with the past to make sense of the present. Fitzgerald's Crack-Up essay has a sort of popularization of Freudian psychoanalysis in the early mid 20th century America.

Fitzgerald make a candid confession as to how he had been cracked up in life : "For seventeen years, with the year of deliberate loafing and resting out in the center — things went on like that, with a new chore only a nice prospect for the next day. — And then, ten years this side of forty-nine, I suddenly realized I had prematurely cracked. But the well-known critic Mark Dolan called the Crack Up essays as "Quasi-Platonic Standardized from of the Crack-Up" that "begins to make more sense. The narrator's distant tone and inclination for generalities are much better suited to reflection or interrogation than to revealation. Similarly, his vague commentary on a past full of 'too much anger and tears' should not necessarily call to mind the now quite detailed biographical picture we have of Fitzgerald in the 1930s. It draws attention to the very absence of personal details and could be seen as a reference to any number of issues explicitly mentioned in the text, such as the narrator's anguish over America's rapidly changing cultural landscape or the sense of persecution he seems to feel in relation in his profession.

In 1932, Fitzgerald's wife Zelda was hospitalized owing to schizophrenic symptoms in Baltalised, Maryland. The novel *Tender Is the Night* echoes this incident of his personal life. In the novel, the hero Dick Diver's wife Nicole is given the substantial space for narration owing to her psychological disintegration. Fitzgerald wrote about the hero, "Dick tried to rest —, the struggle would come presently at home and he might have to sit a long time, restating the universe for her. A "schizophrine" is well named as a split personality — Nicole was alternately a person to whom nothing need be explained and one to whom nothing need be explained. It was necessary to treat her with active and affirmative insistence, keeping the road to reality always open, making the road to escape harder going. But the brilliance the versatility of madness is akin to the resourcefulness of water seeping through, over and around a lake. It requires the united front of many people to work against it. He felt it necessary that this time Nicole cure herself; he wanted to wait until she remembered the other times, and revolted from them. In a tried way, he planned that they would again resume the regime relaxed a year before".

Some recent studies in the "Crack-Up" essays focus on the fact that the rhetorical trend used by Fitzgerald and the rhetorical trend employed by the author persona make the same pieces of creation. Many modern critics tried to study Fitzgerald's complex attitudes towards his writings. To conclude, we may quote from A. Banerjee on the Crack-Up essay: "Fitzgerald underwent a chastening experience in the sense that he was able to analyse his past as a writer in the context of the demands of the present. He came to realize that he would have to change according to the changing circumstances of his life".

(d) Contemporary Social Pictures in "The Crack-Up" Essays

"My own happiness in the past often approached such an ecstasy that I could not share it even with the person dearest to me but had to walk it away in a quiet street and lanes with only fragments of it to distill into little lines in books — and I think that my happiness, or talent self-delusion or what you will, was an exception. It was not the natural thing but his unnatural and natural as the Boom; and my recent experience parallels the wave of despair that swept the nation when the Boom was over". (The Crack-Up/ Part III)

The word "Boom" itself describes the social pictures of America in the 1920s. This decade was the period of a magical developments and miracles with excess in everything in society. Therefore, Fitzgerald defined this decade as "roaring twenties". America became, or at least assumed to become the most powerful nation in the world. But at the same time literature played with eroticism and the whole race went without hedonistic. Without prohibition on alcohol, the younger generation began with the cocktail parties. There were "Boom" also in urban construction and the rapid growth of consumer capitalism made the New York Stock-market soar high. But then came devastating stock market crash in 1929 that followed the Great Depression of 1930s. The thirties were a period that marked the severe economic hardship in America. To say in a, the Boom gone and Doom prevailed.

The theme of The Crack-Up essays are not only the personal story of Fitzgerald, but they are the story of many disappointed youth of the America at the time who at the end of "Boom" played into the world of "Doom". Fitzgerald tottered among irreparable truths and he denied himself the luxury of a halo either of a saint or of a martyr. It was Zelda his wife, who put a ridiculous crown of throws on his Fitzgerald bove it protest and without any grudge. He was a man of humble means and tried to see himself clearly. One of the critics of Fitzgerald, Cioran, commented : "... instead of blessing that darkness as a source of revelation, Fitzgerald dammed it, assimilated it into the degradation and emptied of its weight of knowledge. He went through a Pascalian experience without a Pascalian mind. Like all frivolous people, he dreaded going farther into himself. Yet destiny pushed him to it. He hated to extend his being to its limits, and he reached them despite himself ... It's a second-rate mind that cannot choose between literature and the 'true night of the soul". However, Fitzgerald's Crack Up essays were the candid admission of failure that no other writer of America dared to make it before. Fitzgerald raised his psychological paralysis to the level of a work of art.

Fitzgerald's Crack-Up essays owe its topology of shattered dreams and hopeless despair to the vocabulary of the 1920s finance market with their confident speculation of credits and loans their optimistic growth and state politics, in which an emotional language was used to make out and say manage the reality of larger monetary system, governmence and public reaction. These essay of Fitzgerald view the post-1929 social condition and financial status in the context of large scale bankrupty when saving were brought to contraction and the "Beady eyed man used to see on the community trains from train great next fifteen years back men who did in care whether the world tumbled into tomorrow, a personal it spared and their houses". The contemporary gloomy social picture is quite evident in other work of Fitzgerald also. In 1925 novel *The Great Gatsby*, the doomed hero Jay Gatsby rode the euphoric wave of the roaring twenties; he "believed in the green light, the orgiastic future that year by year recedes before us. It Cluded us then, but that's no matter tomorrow we will run faster, stretch out our arms farther .... And one fine morning — so we bent on, boats against the current, brone back ceaselessly into the past. In his 1920 short stories 'Head and Shoulders' the same tune in of social picture is found.

"Horace and Maria were married early in February. The sensation in academic circles both at Yale and Princeton was tremendous. Horace Tarbox, was at fourteen had been played up in the Sunday magazine sections of Metropolitan newspapers, was throwing over his career, his chance of being or a chorus girl— they made Maria a chorus girl. But like all modern stories it was a four-and-a half day wonder.

Thus, the author persona in Fitzgerald tries to find out his own identity as an individual throughout the journey of his life. The loneliness and anxiety crowd in upon his mind at early mornings, say at three o'clock. He says, "one is not waiting for the fade out of a single sorrow, but rather being an unwilling witness of an execution, the disintegration of one's own personality". Sometimes his identity is evaporated, sometimes the realization that his illusion about the man he had been are all vanished. He becomes the total to the influences of which he had been subjected, the individuals whom he believed to think for him. Thus, Wilson become his intellectual conscience, Hemingway become his artistic conscience, Sap Donahoe became his moral conscience, Murphy became his aesthetic conscience and or young communist became his political conscience. Fitzgerald felt that "there was not an "I" any more - not or basis on which I could organise my self-respect save my limitless capacity for toil that it seemed I possessed no more."

(e) The Crisis of Fitzgerald's "Crack-Up"

Scott Donaldson

Donaldson, Scott, "The Crisis of Fitzgerald's "Crack-Up", in *Twentieth Century Literature*, Vol. 26, No. 2. F. Scott. Issue, Summer (1980) pp. 171-188.

The Crisis of Fitzgerald's "Crack-Up

Scott DONALDSON

I. The Reaction

F. Scott Fitzgerald's three "Crack-Up" articles that ran in *Esquire* for February, March, and April 1936 precipitated an extraordinary response from the magazine's readers. "I get letters from all over," Fitzgerald wrote editor Arnold Gingrich on March 20. These letters came from old friends who wanted to cheer him up, from total strangers who recognized something of their own plight in Fitzgerald's account of emotional exhaustion, and most of all from other writers, among them James Boyd, John Dos Passes, Ernest Hemingway, Nancy Hoyt, John O'Hara, Marjorie Kinnan Rawlings, G. B. Stern, Julian Street, and Alexander Woollcott. As O'Hara put it in an April letter, "I suppose you get comparatively little mail these days that does not dwell at greater or less length on your Esquire pieces, and I guess few of the writers resist, as I am resisting, the temptation to go into their own troubles for purposes of contrast." (O'Hara then revealed that he had recently been jilted by his girl and had picked up a dose of clap on the rebound.)

The very nature of Fitzgerald's articles called for some response. Here a well-known writer was admitting in print that he had cracked like a plate and lost much of the vitality that made him successful. Furthermore, at the end of the second article, Fitzgerald openly appealed for reader reaction. His story might not be of general interest, yet if anyone wanted more, he announced, there was plenty left. But perhaps his readers had already had enough. If so, he hoped they'd let him know.

The correspondence that found its way back to Fitzgerald varied enormously in tone. Much of it sympathetically proposed solutions to his dilemma. Some letter-writers suggested God, some Alcoholics Anonymous, some a rendezvous. Others recounted their own troubles, delivered pep talks, tried to jolly him up. More than a few thought he should never have begun the series of autobiographical pieces at all. (Five more articles followed the three about the "Crack-Up" in *Esquire*, but the later pieces were not so painfully defeatist as (the earlier ones.) "People have received this *Esquire* article ("An Author's Mother") with mingled feeling," he wrote Beatrice Dance in September 1936,"—not a few of them think it was a terrific mistake to have written any of them from Crack-Up. On the other hand, I get innumerable 'fan letters' and requests to republish them in the *Reader's Digest*, and several anthologist's requests, which I prudently refused.[4] As he'd acknowledged at the beginning of "Pasting It Together" (the second "Crack-Up" article)[5], there were "always those to whom all self-revelation is contemptible, unless it ends with a noble thanks to the gods for the Unconquerable Soul."[6] There were also those who could not resist the opportunity to preach at Fitzgerald. "Please write me," he asked Max Perkins in February 1937, "you are about the only friend who does not see fit to incorporate a moral lesson, especially since the Crack-Up stuff. Actually I hear from people in Sing Sing & Joliet all comforting & advising me."[7]

Certainly "The Crack-Up" essays conveyed a strong impression of personal depression. The New Yorker's "Talk of the Town" dismissed them with its usual snide superiority. "F. Scott Fitzgerald has been telling, in *Esquire*, how sad he feels in middle life," the item began, and went on to refer to his "picturesque despondency."[6] *The San Francisco Chronicle* observed in similar vein that the "gentleman in question is being a little too sorry for himself," but acknowledged that one could "hardly help being interested in what he has to say," the more so since he seemed to strike a common chord, and his essays went far "to explain the spiritual troubles of many another member of the almost-lost generation."[9]

Such friends as Margaret Turnbull and Marie Hamm agreed. "Your story is a mental snapshot of a rather universal experience," Mrs. Turnbull wrote after reading his first article. All of us end up more or less defeated," but since so many shared this experience, Fitzgerald would discover "a chain of people, stretching around the world, to catch hold of [his] hands."[10] One hand that reached out was that of Scott's first girl in St. Paul, Marie Hersey Hamm. "Cheer up, darling, life begins at forty! she wrote early in October, responding both to the Esquire articit a to the account, in *Time*, of his disastrous 40th birthday interview .. rr Michel Mok for the New York Post. Mrs. Hamm granted that Fitzgerald had probably gone "on a more prolonged binge than the rest of us, and that therefore his "hang-over, awakening, or what have you was that much more oppressive. But Life, she insisted, was pretty sweb, especially when you considered the alternative. Among their mutual friends, for instance, Joe Ordway was in a sanitorium and Theodore Schultze had died the week before. "When you're dead, you're dead, my pet. so why not enjoy it while you're here. [11]Bob and Rave Sylvester on The New York News extended their hands from out of the blue, first itemizing reasons why Fitzgerald couldn't quit now (he was too old to go into a tailspin, he was the only writer in the world who understood kids, he'd deprive Bob Sylvester of his saloon argument that Fitzgerald's novels would outlive Caesar's Gallic Wars). They concluded by praising Tender Is the Night and wishing that the man who wrote it would get well and happy and back to work soon!

Mostly, Fitzgerald refused to be cheered up by such correspondence. It was nice of Marie Hamm to try. "However, child," he told her, "life is more complicated than that." To the Sylvesters he sent a more discouraged reply:

"The thing is this: that you go along thinking, this is the way things are, and that is all right; you go along at the same time saying that this is the way things should be, but you are not sure; and you keep your tongue in your cheek about how things will be, but the safest prophecy' is the most dismal.

Now, second: You go along thinking that you will get by no matter when you think that the methods you have used are all right. Then you come up. Because the first two don't fit together, and you never thought you had character, anyhow.[13]

Some people thought he had demonstrated his lack of character by publishing the pieces in the first place. To Sara Murphy, for example, Fitzgerald seemed so wrapped up in himself as to be unable to sympathize with others. Did Scott really, honestly think that "life was something you dominated if you were any good?" That kind of arrogance brought an incident to mind:

"I remember once your saying to me—in Montana at Harry's Hat, you & Dotty (Parker) were talking about your disappointments, & you turned turned to me and said: I don't suppose you have ever known despair? I remember it so well as I was furious, & thought my god the man thinks no one knows despair who isn't a writer & can describe it. This is my feeling about your articles.

John Dos Passos also proposed that Fitzgerald stop regarding his own novel. Christ, man, how do you find time in the middle of the general conflagration to worry about all that stuff? . .. We're living in one of the damnedest tragic moments in history—if you want to go to pieces I think it's absolutely O.K. but I think you ought to write a first-rate novel about it (and you probably will) instead of spilling it in little pieces for Arnold Gingrich—"

The important thing, to Dos Passos and other writer-friends, was that Fitzgerald should continue to do his work. "Katy & I ... wish like hell you could find some happy way of getting that magnificent working apparatus of yours to work darkening paper; which is its business," as Dos put it in another letter. Even if he remained unhappy, Fitzgerald ought to turn that sorrow to literary account. "I suppose you know that nothing is wasted," Marjorie

Kinnan Rawlings asserted. "The hell you've been through isn't wasted. All you have to do, ever, is to forget everything and turn that terrible, clear white light you possess, on the minds and emotions of the people it stirs you to write about." Ernest Hemingway had offered much the same advice after reading Tender Is the Night and detecting traces of self-pity in the portrayal of Dick Diver. Forget your personal tragedy, he told Fitzgerald. "But when you get the damned hurt use it—don't cheat with it." Neither of them were tragic characters. They were only writers, and what they should do was write.

Hemingway did not mean, however, that Fitzgerald should bleed all over the page. "The Crack-Up" articles struck him as a despicable whining in public. His old friend Scott had become the Maxie Baer of writers, he wrote Max Perkins, sunk to the canvas in the "shamelessness of defeat." In "The Snows of Kilimanjaro," which appeared in the August 1936 *Esquire*, Hemingway dismissed Fitzgerald openly. Poor Scott Fitzgerald" had been "wrecked," Ernest wrote, by his worship of the rich. When Fitzgerald objected, Hemingway explained that since Scott had written himself off in "The Crack-Up" he figured it was open season on him? It must have been something of the same savage distaste for public confession that inspired syndicated columnist Westbrook Pegler's ill-spirited obituary of Fitzgerald, whose death recalled to Pegler "memories of a queer band of undisciplined and self-indulgent brats who were determined not to pull their weight in the boat and wanted the world to drop everything and sit down and bawl with them."

Though he did not share the vehemence of Hemingway or Pegler, the gentlemanly Perkins was also embarrassed by "The Crack-Up" articles. Parading one's troubles in public simply wasn't done. The essays constituted the author's "indecent invasion of his own privacy. As an editor, therefore, Perkins faced a problem when Fitzgerald proposed on March 25, 1936 that his autobiographical magazine writing might be stitched together into a good and saleable book. Perkins had earlier discouraged this idea, but since "the interest in this *Esquire* series has been so big," Fitzgerald pointed out, "I thought you might reconsider the subject.. ." Perkins replied tactfully that he'd much prefer "a reminiscent book—not autobiographical but reminiscent. I do not think the Esquire pieces ought to be published alone. But as for an autobiographical book which would comprehend what is in them, I would be very much for it." It would need integration, however, and should not be a mere collection of articles.[24] Three months later Gilbert Seldes echoed the point in a letter to Fitzgerald. Collections of scattered articles rarely made sense or money, Seldes observed, and then went on to make an argument for the book of reminiscence Perkins had favored:

"...more important, Scott, is that you seem more and more to me an essential figure in America and sooner or later you will have to say your complete say, not only in fiction, but in the facts about yourself and the part you played at the beginning and what you think of it now.[25]

By the fall of 1936, Fitzgerald had abandoned any idea of collecting "The Crack-Up" articles. Both Perkins and agent Harold Ober had by then indicated that the articles were doing real damage to his reputation as a writer. "My Hollywood deal...," he wrote Beatrice Dance in September, "was seriously compromised by their general tone. It seems to have implied to some people that I was a complete moral and artistic bankrupt." The Mok interview might never have come about, he felt, if he hadn't composed "those indiscreet Esquire articles." As a consequence he began disavowing them. They were not to be taken too seriously, he told Hamilton Basso. Later he withheld the articles from Sheikh Graham lor some time before showing her the tearsheets with the admonition, "I shouldn't have written these."

When Edmund Wilson began assembling the volume of Fitzgerald's non-fiction and others' critical acclaim which emerged in 1945 as The Crack-Up, he encountered some opposition from both Perkins and Ober. As early as February 1941 Wilson had suggested to Perkins that "The Crack Up should be brought out in book form."I hated it when it came out, just as you did, Wilson remarked, "but I have found several intelligent people that think highly of it. There was more truth and sincerity in it, I suppose, than we realized at the time. He wanted it published in a book himself, and after all I dare say it is a part of the real Fitzgerald record." "These were excellent reasons for Scribner's to publish such a book, but Perkins remained adamant. Eventually Wilson took his project to New Directions, but not before he'd lobbied on its behalf with Fitzgerald's financial executor, John Biggs. He intended to call his book The Crack-Up, editor Wilson explained, not because he was enamored of the title, but because Glenway Wescott's appreciation is largely based on The Crack-Up, and ... if you read The Crack-Up through, you realize that it is not a discreditable confession but an account of a kind of crisis that many men of Scott's generation have gone through, and that in the end he sees a way to live by application to his work. "I hope," Wilson added, "that you can counteract with your influence any influence that Ober and Max Perkins may have had on Scottie, and that you can allay her misgivings.

(f) The Circumstances

How did Fitzgerald come to write his three "gloom articles," as he referred to them in his Ledger? He finished "The Crack-Up" itself in October 1935, "Pasting It Together" and "Handle with Care" in December. At that time he was suffering through an extremely low period in his life, during which he attempted to drive off with liquor and sex the awareness that Zelda would never be wholly well, the realization that his earning power had drastically diminished while the bills mounted ever higher, and the sense that he'd let his life and his talent waste away. In 1935-1936, he observed, "all my products were direges & elegies."

When Arnold Gingrich came calling in Baltimore one day in the spring of 1935, he found Fitzgerald in a "ratty old bathrobe" moaning about having to write a story of young love for the *Saturday Evening Post*. He couldn't do such stories with enthusiasm anymore, and the idea of producing one brought up his "cold george." "Well, why not write about that?" Gingrich suggested, then thought no more of the matter until, in the fall, the first of the three "Crack-Up" pieces arrived on his deck.

Fitzgerald had spent the intervening summer in Asheville, North Carolina, carrying on a reckless affair with a married woman and drinking vast quantities of alcohol. Laura Guthrie (later Laura Hearne), who was his "secretary" (that is, his always-to-be-available companion, good listener, potential conquest, and occasional typist) that summer, began by admiring and feeling sorry for her employer and ended in near-disgust. In the exhaustive diary she kept of those days, Mrs. Guthrie set down her initial impression of Fitzgerald:

"He is completely alone because no persons are near to him, and he has no religion to comfort him. He makes me think of a lost soul, wandering in purgatory—sometimes hell. He tries so hard to drown it out with drinking and sex. Sometimes in the heights of these moments he forgets for a brief time—then it all comes back in overwhelming force. "Life is not happy," as he says. It isn't for him. He said it was a good thing he was not a rich man or he would have been dead before now (killing himself with indulgences!) but that the necessity of doing work had kept him going. Now he hopes that life will continue to be just endurable, which will only be if he keeps enough health to work.

One can detect here the humble secretary parroting the thoughts of the great man, but by the end of the summer—after she had been exposed to every sort of indignity, including lying to cover up Fitzgerald's affair with Beatrice Dance and witnessing his daily attempt to achieve oblivion through drink—Mrs. Guthrie was only hoping to get rid of him. She finally managed to do so on Friday the 13th of September, when Scott, who had switched from beer and ale to gin a week earlier, broke down physically and allowed himself to be placed in the local hospital. When she arrived at his hotel room that morning, Mrs. Guthrie found empty glasses everywhere and Fitzgerald himself in terrible condition, with bloodshot eyes, drawn lips, skin raw from eczema, twitching leg muscles and a distorted look about the face that made her realize he couldn't last much longer. "My nerves are going," he told her. "I'm about to break.' He could not work at all. He wept, as he often had that summer. He pretended he was having a heart attack. Then, though it didn't seem fair that she should have to get him to the hospital, Mrs. Guthrie helped her invalid pack up his filthy clothes and get dressed so that he could march through the lobby and check out as if he were on his way to the train. Upon depositing him at the hospital she "felt like a kid out of school," his responsibility over. Nothing could ever happen to get me to put my head in this noose again,' she noted in her diary. "At first I had thought that I could save him and help him to write steadily and really be his good angel, but I have decided that no one can be this...".

The collapse in Asheville was Fitzgerald's fourth breakdown from liquor in the space of about two years, he told Mrs. Guthrie.[36] Within a month he had dried out enough to write "The Crack-Up," but another year and more would elapse before his long spell of despondency and drunkenness came to an end. By mid-1937, he was able to confide most of the truth to his notebooks:

What got me in the two years mess that reached its lowest point in the fall of 1936 [when he was again in Asheville under constant care by nurses, and attempted suicide twice] was the usual combination of circumstances. A prejudiced enemy might say it was all drink, a fond Mama might say it was a run of ill-luck, a banker might say it was not providing for the future in better days, a psychologist might say it was a nervous collapse— it was perhaps partly all these things—the effect was to prevent me from doing my work at the very age when presumably one is at the height of one's powers. My life looked like a hopeless mess there for a while and the point was I didn't want it to be better. I had completely ceased to give a good god-damn.

(g) The Art

When *The Crack-Up* emerged as a book in 1945, several critics celebrated its honesty. Lionel Trilling hailed Fitzgerald's "heroic self-awareness." Glenway Wescott praised his candor. Andrews Wanning detected a desperate effort at self-disclosure." In some ways, the essays were unusually candid. "The Crack-Up" accurately reflected Fitzgerald's tendency toward sadness for example. "Please don't be depressed, Zelda had written him in 1931. "Nothing is sad about you except your sadness and the frayed places in your pink kimono and that you care so much about everything ... O my love, I love you so—and I want you to be happy." But her husband was temperamentally unsuited to happiness. Hemingway's "instinct (was) toward megalomania," he later commented, "and mine toward melancholy."

Yet Fitzgerald was far from totally forthcoming in the articles for *Esquire*. One feels on reading them, as Alfred Kazin saw, "that something is being persistently withheld, that the author is somehow offering us certain facts in exchange for the right to keep others to himself."[43] In fact The Crack-Up" is surprisingly short of that kind of concrete evidence which lends conviction to the greatest confessional writing.[44] The thing most conspicuously left out was, naturally, Fitzgerald's alcoholism— "naturally because as both Wescott and Malcolm Cowley have observed, denying that one has a drinking problem constitutes one of the symptoms of the disease.[45] Still, it was disingenuous of Fitzgerald to dismiss the issue in the first of his "Crack-Up" articles. There he referred to William Seabrook's book about alcoholism which "tells, with some pride and a movie ending, of how he became a public charge." Seabrook's nervous system had collapsed, and so, admitted Fitzgerald, had his own, but not because of drink: "the present writer was not so entangled," he lied, "— having at the time not tasted so much as a glass of beer for six months."

Such denials did not convince everyone. John V. A. Weaver, another writer associated with the Jazz Age, found the first two Esquire articles disturbing, since they described so exactly what had happened to him. And what was that? "I can't drink a drop," he wrote Fitzgerald. "I can only sit impotent, day by day, and see a strange world career by—a world in which I have no place."[47] Weaver mailed his letter in February 1936, while George Martin (who did not know Fitzgerald) waited until after the publication of "An Alcoholic Case" in February 1937 to offer his assurance that he'd been in the same boat. "From the stuff you write in *Esquire* you seem to be having one hell of a time," Martin began. "If it's true ... please know that I've lived all through it—will to die, its, friends gone, money gone, job gone, self-respect gone, guts gone... everything." He then suggested that Fitzgerald get hold of Peabody's Common Sense of Drinking.

This letter obviously struck a nerve, for Fitzgerald answered by external reasons for his malady. Martin gently chided him in reply: "Certainly, as you say, the cause precedes the curse but it is also true that the old ego breeds rationalizations like guinea pigs."

Indeed, much of "The Crack-Up" reads like a rationalization of Fitzgerald's breakdown and the three articles represent more an apologia than a confession. The blame for his crack-up, Fitzgerald implies, lies not within himself but elsewhere: the deficient genes he was bequeathed, the contemporary climate of materialism and insincerity even the growth of motion pictures which threatened to put fiction writers out of business.

By the middle of 1937, when he was drafting his autobiographical essay on "Early Success," Scott had matured enough to recognize this self-deception. There, in a passage he later cut out of the essay, Fitzgerald compared himself unfavorably with his own father, a man who had failed without seeking scapegoats. This passage was intended to accompany the discussion of the relative importance of will and fate in determining success which appears in the published essay as "The man who arrives young believes that he exercises his will because his star is shining. The man who only asserts himself at thirty has a balanced idea of what will power and fate have each contributed...." Then, in part of the typescript he later deleted, came the following, with Fitzgerald's lined-through corrections indicated in italics:

It is easy enough from half a century's perspective to gloss Fitzgerald's reference to "several years of private misfortune"—these were the years of Zelda's final relapse into schizophrenia and his own immersion in drink. But what was the "comparatively small blow" that toppled him into the slough of despond? The dramatic logic of "The Crack-Up" demanded that some immediate cause be located, and so in the first of his essays he indicated that it was a piece of unexpected good news from his doctor—a reprieve from an earlier death sentence—that led him to crack like an old plate. Such an event may have happened, but no biographer has documented it. Probably, Fitzgerald was exaggerating his own situation in order to contrast the dread loss of vitality (a bankruptcy that resulted, he wrote, from mortgaging himself "physically and spiritually up to the hilt") with the comparatively unimportant "small gift of life given back.... ' In the remaining "Crack-Up" essays, significantly, he dropped all references to this medical reprieve. In "Pasting It Together," he cited three specific blows that led up to his breakdown:

dropping out of Princeton because of ill health (he does not mention his academic difficulties), temporarily losing Zelda because of lack of money, and suffering an unspecified, more violent third blow that "cut off the sun last spring."[52]

Obviously and quite understandably, Fitzgerald was telling less than the whole truth about himself and his family. A similar reticence led him to eliminate almost all names from his articles, though he does acknowledge Edmund Wilson as his "intellectual conscience." In "The Crack-Up" Fitzgerald was working in a genre new to him. "Although presented as autobiography," Kenneth Eble has commented, the articles "have the air of highly wrought and intensely felt fiction." But that is not the case exactly, for how often in Fitzgerald's short stories would one find references to the Bible, to William Ernest Henley, to Wordsworth and Keats, to Lenin and Dickens and Tolstoy, to Spinoza, to Descartes, to the Euganean Hills? And how often would Fitzgerald as a writer of fiction allow metaphor to substitute for concrete action, as it does so often in "The Crack-Up" essays? Instead of providing specific detail, Fitzgerald compares himself to a cracked plate, a beggar carrying the "tin cup of self-pity," a bankrupt who had overdrawn his account, a lecturer about to lose his audience, an empty shell, a conjurer fresh out of tricks, a Negro lady cutting out a rival, a Negro retainer pretending to jollity, and a dog who will remain subservient if thrown a bone from time to time.[53] Saying what one is like provides an alternative to saying outright what one actually is. Like the wealth of learned references, it was a form of evasion.

The tone of the articles varied from the tough wise-guyism of "All rather inhuman and undernourished, isn't it? Well, that, children, is the true sign of cracking up" in the first essay to the ornate confusion of "The dullest platitude monger or the most unscrupulous Rasputin who can influence the destinies of many people must have some individuality so the question became one of finding why and where I had changed, where was the leak through which, unknown to myself, my enthusiasm and my vitality had been steadily and prematurely trickling away" in the third. Fitzgerald was searching for a form, but he had not quite found it. Re-reading "The Crack-Up" today, one is inclined to share the ambivalent reaction of the woman who wrote Fitzgerald that she found it hard to believe his articles really touched the depths of tragedy, yet they were "so convincing as to leave little room for doubt that the author had at some time lived those bitternesses and depressions." The source of this ambivalence, according to William Barrett, lay in the excessive artfulness of the essays "The Crack-Up," he wrote,

is a frightening thing to read: rapid, brilliant, but also jerky and almost metallically tense in tone, as if still vibrating with the receding hysteria of the breakdown. No doubt Fitzgerald, writing for *Esquire* magazine, felt he had to jazz up his material, but, even with allowance made for this, these pieces leave the impression that the author is still seeing life much too much in literary and dramatic terms. A man writing of his own human defeat and failure ought to have passed beyond "literature" altogether, even to the point of risking a matter-of-factness that might appear prosy and plodding....

It is a dangerous business, this prescribing the correct technique for authors, but a more matter-of-fact approach would, it seems to me also, have given Fitzgerald's essays that authority and verisimilitude they now lack. In fact, apology masquerading as confession may well represent, in Alfred Kazin's words, "the best possible device for not revealing" the truth.

As it stands, "The Crack-Up" tells its truths only between the lines. It is not about nervous exhaustion, emotional bankruptcy, or even an alcoholic breakdown. The subject of "The Crack-Up is Fitzgerald's misanthropy, and the self-hatred behind it. All the essays, but especially the first and last, deal with the author's attempted escape from people—more particularly his escape from that large group of people to whom he has felt obliged to give something of himself. He has given too much in the past. He will, he says, give no more.

When the writing touches on this subject, it achieves a vividness missing elsewhere. Upon hearing the "grave sentence" of his doctor, Fitzgerald writes in the first article, he "wanted to be absolutely alone" and so cut himself off from ordinary cares." Instead he sat around making lists. "It was not," he reveals, "an unhappy time." Then came the crack-up and with it the realization that "for a long time I had not liked people and things, but only followed the rickety old pretense of liking." In his casual relations— with an editor, a tobacco seller, the child of a friend"— he had merely done what was expected. Even with love, he had been going through the motions. He had, in short, been guilty of emotional insincerity for some time, yet he does not publicly blame himself. Instead, he transfers his self-disgust into distaste for most other human beings.

He still admires the looks of middle-western Scandinavian blondes. He likes "doctors and girl children up to the age of about thirteen and well-brought-up boy children from about eight years old on." He likes old men and Katherine Hepburn's face on the screen, and Miriam Hopkins' face, and old friends if he only has to see them once a year. But there is a larger category of people he has come to detest:

"I couldn't stand the sight of Celts, English, Politicians, Strangers, Virginians, Negroes (light or dark), Hunting People, all retail clerks, and middlemen in general, all writers (I avoided writers very carefully because they can perpetuate trouble as no one else can)—and all the classes as classes and most of them, as members of their class...."

Under the pressure of his crack-up Fitzgerald withdrew from contact with the real world into a period of "vacuous quiet" during which he was forced to think for himself. He then discovered, according to the second article, that he had never done this before. All his ideas had been borrowed from Edmund Wilson and from four other unnamed men, one of whom, his "artistic conscience," was surely Ernest Hemingway. Not only had he given too freely of himself to people he didn't care about, but he had submerged his mental development by passively adopting the ideas of others. There was no "I" any more, Fitzgerald concluded, no basis on which he could organize his self-respect.

The third article, "Handle with Care," picks up this theme. Unlike I escartes. Fitzgerald's motto had been, "I felt-therefore I was." He had, in fact, felt too much, and so he decides that if he wishes to survive he must cease "any attempts to be a person-to be kind, just or generous." Instead he rather cynically resolves to develop a false smile to win the favor of those who might be of use to him, and otherwise to cultivate the habit of saying no in a voice that will make "people feel that far from being welcome they are not even tolerated....

In the last paragraph of this last "Crack-Up" article, Fitzgerald located the source of his malady in two telling comparisons. For too long he had concentrated on pleasing others, and in the process neglected his own development:

... And just as the laughing stoicism which has enabled the American Negro to endure the intolerable conditions of his existence has cost him his sense of the truth—so in my case there is a price to pay.

Now that he has determined to change, life will no longer be as pleasant as it once was. He is a different sort of dog now, one who no longer likes "the postman, nor the grocer, nor the editor, nor the cousin's husband ... and the sign Cave Canem is hung permanently just above my door." He will only lick your hand now, Fitzgerald says, if you throw him a bone. This cynicism, like much cynicism, is directed against the self. In repudiating a past in which he has too often played the fawning servant or the lovable lap dog, Fitzgerald was implicitly condemning himself and preparing the way for a fresh start.

Despite these protestations, Fitzgerald never became really anti-social. But he did reorder his priorities so that doing his work and fulfilling his obligations came ahead of his drive to charm other people. During the Hollywood years he seems finally to have achieved a sense of self-respect, a term which Joan Didion has defined in a passage that uncannily echoes the theme of "The Crack-Up":

are on the one hand forced to despise those who have so few resources as to consort with us, so little perception as to remain blind to our fatal weaknesses. On the other, we are peculiarly in thrall to everyone we see, curiously determined to live out—since our self-image is untenable—their false notions of us. We flatter ourselves by thinking this compulsion to please others an attractive trait: a gist for imaginative empathy, evidence of our willingness to give. Of course I will play Francesca to your Paolo, Helen Keller to anyone's Anne Sullivan: no expectation is too misplaced, no role too ludicrous. At the mercy of those we cannot but, hold in contempt, we play roles doomed to failure before they are begun, each defeat generating fresh despair at the urgency of divining and meeting the next demand made upon us.

It is the phenomenon sometimes called "alienation from self." In its advanced stages, we no longer answer the telephone, because someone might want something; that we could say no without drowning in self-reproach is an idea alien to this game. Every encounter demands too much, tears the nerves, drains the will....

This "alienation from self" lies behind Fitzgerald's breakdown, and behind his announced misanthropy. The very process of putting words down on paper helped free him from that alienation. The insightful Perkins, who maintained that no one "would write those articles if they were really true," came to the conclusion "that in some deep way, when he wrote those articles, Scott must have been thinking that things would be different with him." Other readers agreed that the articles must surely have a purgative effect. He'd be willing to bet, Burton Rascoe observed after seeing the first two essays, that Fitzgerald was "already feeling immensely better . . . self-confident and creative again." "You've been finding out a lot of things that have hurt like hell," Julian Street told Fitzgerald, "and at the end of it you'll be grown up ... a bigger and better man and a bigger and better writer for it." In replying to Street on February 24, 1936, Fitzgerald acknowledged that since the intensity of despair had moderated somewhat, he could see that writing the articles "was a form of catharsis but at the time of writing them what I said seemed absolutely real." He could also see, he added defensively, that "an unfriendly critic might damn the series as the whining of a spoilt baby," but wasn't that true of most poetry?

It is true of Fitzgerald not only that his characters are modeled on himself but that he sometimes becomes his characters after the fact. Thus his retreat to Asheville, Tryon, Hendersonville in North Carolina during the two years of his personal depression virtually repeated Dick Diver drifting among the small towns of upstate New York. Like Diver too, Fitzgerald had to abandon his goal of becoming an "an entire man ... with an opulent American touch, a sort of combination of J.P. Morgan. Topham Beauclerk and St. Francis of Assisi" He will now be "a writer only," he announces in the last of the "Crack-Up" articles, just as Dick: Diver finally became only a doctor, no longer a scientist or entertainer or bon vivant.The difference is that Diver faded away, while Fitzgerald emerged from his fallen estate to live a useful and productive four years.

Fitzgerald referred to the "Crack-Up" articles in his ledger as biography, not autobiography.' This apparent slip of the pen, as Robert Sklar has observed, revealed the "essential truth" that the Scott Fitzgerald described in the essays was not the same as the man who wrote about him. I don't know whether those articles of mine in *Esquire*— the 'Crack-Up' series—represented a real nervous break-down," Fitzgerald remarked in July 1939. "In retrospect it seems more of a spiritual 'change of life'—and a most unwilling one... " "Transformation" might be an even better term than "change of life," for in "The Crack-Up". Fitzgerald sloughed off the skin of the old Irish charmer and determined to let work instead of play dominate the time left to him. The articles hardly achieve what Trilling called a "heroic awareness." It took courage to say as much as he did, but Fitzgerald left too much only hinted at and blamed too many external forces for his predicament to be adjudged a hero of self-revelation. Despite the false leads and evasions, however, Fitzgerald did uncover more of himself between the lines of these articles, and particularly of the last article, than anywhere else in his 'works. And, though the benefits did not surface immediately, the process did him good. "The Crack-Up" does not measure up to the best confessional writing, but it had something of the same therapeutic effect on the man who set it down on paper.

(h) F. Scott Fitzgerald: The Representative Author of his Time in America

Francis Scott Fitzgerald was the multitalented genius in American literature. He was a novelist, essayist, screenplay writer and short story writer. He is rightly called the represetative author of American literature. His well acclaimed novels and short stories depict the flamboyance and excess of the jazz age—or term coined by Fitzgerald himself to describe the particular period of 1920s.

In his famous novel "The Great Gatsby" he conveyed the sense of hope American promised to the youths of the twenties and finally their disappointment and disillusionment offer the great crash at Wall Street in 1929 following the great depression. His novel "The Great Gatsby" and "Tender is the Night" convey the message of new found prosperity, consumerism and shifting sexual moods of the American society.

The result of a boom based on illusion and euphoria was matched by an inner ruin in the society that affected the thousands of youths in America and all suffered crack up problem like Fitzgerald. All lost their vitality, an exhaustion of nervous energy, universal pessimism captured the young minds and all were heading towards a morbid attraction to nothingness. There were lots of examples that touched the conscience of many and hunt many. Harry Crosby committed suicide, Edmund Wilson suffered a nervous breakdown, and many were suffering from general pathological crisis. Carl Van Doren was suffering from "private depression" as Fitzgerald suffered himself. The collapse of Wall Street did not affect him. Even his income in 1930 was larger than in 1929. In spite of that he suffered depression and that was due to "lethargy, soreness and intentness together."

Once Fitzgerald had secret Yen for a Scandinavian Blonde who used to sit on the porches in St. Paul's but as he suffered economic crisis, he couldn't proceed farther with the affair and as a result of it in his latter life, he fear the sight of Celts, English, politicians, strangers, Virginians, Negroes (light or dark), Hunting people, or retail clerk, middlemen in general and all writers. He avoided writers because they can perpetuate trouble as no one else can.

The Boom of the 1920 did not last long because in 1929 Wall Street collapsed and Great Depression hit the Americans. The gorgeousness of the Roaring Twenties was replaced by misery, deprivation and misfortune of the Depression and Financial Collapse. Lots of people lost their employment resulting permanent breakdown and crack up in their life. People ever lost their homes, banks were closed down and consumerism was totally went into deep trouble. Consumer economy faced an unnatural halt. The Federal Government of Herbert Hoover could not manage the situation with any substantial steps and the people of America wanted to change their Government. And at this juncture, in 1933, F.D. Roosevelt became the 32nd President of America. Fitzgerald's personal crises as well as the burden of making of American society which was breaking down had an ironical impact on the author's mind and he was compelled to look back at the past as an unnatural thing that in comparison made the current situation more pathetic. Fitzgerald's self-confessional essay became a chronicle of an entire society and its generation who were "cracked up" in the same way as Fitzgerald. It was evident that the booming bubble of 1920s came into big "naught".

Fitzgerald also mentioned about the booming film industry of Hollywood. According to Fitzgerald, film industry was "the strongest and supplest medium for carrying thought and emotion from one human being to another. He believed that movies projected nothing but the most obvious of emotions. The fall of Hollywood was rather his own defeat; defeat of his ideals on which he built his matured life. It was rather a nightmare to him when he witnessed that his dearest 'cosmos' was taken over by a grosser power; as a result he lost his nerves and he cracked up like or cracked plate. This personal experience became the universal in the context of American society which was affected by "grosser powers" that can been as "an archaeology of American desire".

When "The Crack Up" essays appeared in 1936 in the *Esquire* Journal, the readers found them to be purely confessional and autobiographical. But before that, his novel "The Great Gatsby had already opened the genre of the confessional. He established that genre of confessional... confession for life, confession for society, confession for tradition, in a single sentence, confession for contemporary society. Fitzgerald truly represented the age for which he wrote and to which he belonged. The autobiographical anxiety in Fitzgerald is always simultaneously historical in nature. "Sad mood" of Fitzgerald represents the "Sad mood" of America and his own "depression" becomes the "Great Depression" for the Nation. This Tryptich essay-series reveal the flowing image of the American Nation that has taken a gloomy shape after the Great Crash of 1929 and faced the Great Depression.

3

Dry September

William Faulkner (1897-1962)

William Cuthbert Faulkner was born on 25th September, 1897 at New Albany, Mississippi, United States. He was a multi-talented American writer who wrote novels, short stories, screenplays, poetry, essays and a play also. Some of his notable novels are *The Sound and The Fury* (1929), *As I Lay Dying* (1930), *Absalom, Absalom!* (1936), *Light In August* (1932), *Sanctuary* (1931), *The Reivers* (1962) etc. The movies he screenplayed include *The Big Sleep*, *To Have and Have Not*, *As I Lay Dying*, *Today We Live*, *The Long, Hot Summer* etc. And his short stories measure a variety of range that includes A Rose for Emily, Barn Burning, Dry September, That Evening Sun, Knight's Gambit etc.

William Faulkner is regarded as one of the greatest writers of the twentieth century. He is remembered for the noted technique of writing—the stream of consciousness technique. He has also a depth of characterisation and range of topic. He received Nobel Prize literature in 1949. This great literature of America is associated with the modernist and Southern gothic literary movements. Faulkner also received Pulitzer prize for fiction in 1955 and 1963. In 1951 and 1955 he received National Book Award.

Faulkner evolved a complicated style with Gothic elements. His writing style includes the extremely long sentences embedding with complex subordinate parts. This great modern author of America died on 6 July, 1962 at Byhalia, Mississippi, U.S.A.

An Introduction to the Story

Dry September was published in January, 1931 in Scribner's Magazine and was republished in the Collection of Faulkner's short story in the same year. It is the story of a rumour that a Nigger, Will Mayes, raped a white woman, Miss Minnie Cooper. The story explores the racial conflict in the U.S.A. specially in the Southern America and the tragic effect of rumour in the life of a black man in the hands of white.

The main character of the story is Will Mayes who is murdered by a group of white mob with no reason. McLendon is a white vigilante, whose gun, hat, handcuffs and experience as a military commander gave him a superior position among the general folks. *Dry September* as a short story, is a devastating critique of the society and culture of the American South and highlights the racial conflicts between the white and the black with social superiority of the former at Jefferson, Mississippi, the fictional town where inhuman murder of the black man takes place.

Dry September

WILLIAM FAULKNER

I

Through the bloody September twilight, aftermath of sixty-two rainless days, it had gone like a fire in dry grass—the rumor, the story, whatever it was. Something about Miss Minnie Cooper and a Negro. Attacked, insulted, frightened: none of them, gathered in the barber shop on that Saturday evening where the ceiling fan stirred, without freshening it, the vitiated air, sending back upon them, in recurrent surges of stale pomade and lotion, their own stale breath and odors, knew exactly what had happened.

"Except it wasn't Will Mayes," a barber said. He was a man of middle age; a thin, sand-colored man with a mild face, who was shaving a client. "I know Will Mayes. He's a good nigger. And I know Miss Minnie Cooper, too."

"What do you know about her?' a second barber said.

"Who is she?" the client said. "A young girl?"

"No," the barber said. "She's about forty, I reckon. She aint married.

That's why 1 dont believe—"

"Believe, hell!" a hulking youth in a sweat-stained silk shirt said.

"Wont you take a white woman's word before a nigger's?"

"I dont believe Will Mayes did it," the barber said. "I know Will Mayes."

"Maybe you know who did it, then. Maybe you already got him out of town, you damn niggerlover."

"I don't believe anybody did anything. I don't believe anything happened. I leave it to you fellows if them ladies that get old without getting married don't have notions that a man cant—"

"Then you are a hell of a white man," the client said. He moved under the cloth. The youth had sprung to his feet.

"You dont?" he said. "Do you accuse a white woman of lying?"

The barber held the razor poised above the half-risen client. He did not look around.

"It's this durn weather," another said. "It's enough to make a man do anything. Even to her."

Nobody laughed. The barber said in his mild, stubborn tone: "I aint accusing nobody of nothing. I just know and you fellows know how a woman that never—"

"You damn niggerlover!" the youth said.

"Shut up, Butch," another said. "We'll get the facts in plenty of time to act."

"Who is? Who's getting them?" the youth said. "Facts, hell! I—"

"You're a fine white man," the client said. "Aint you?" In his frothy beard he looked like a desert rat in the moving pictures. "You tell them, Jack," he said to the youth. "If there aint any white men in this town, you can count on me, even if I aint only a drummer and a stranger."

"That's right, boys," the barber said. "Find out the truth first. I know Will Mayes."

"Well, by God!" the youth shouted. "To think that a white man in this town—"

"Shut up, Butch," the second speaker said. "We got plenty of time.'

The client sat up. He looked at the speaker. "Do you claim that anything excuses a nigger attacking a white woman? Do you mean to tell me you are a white man and you'll stand for it? You better go back North where you came from. The South dont want your kind here."

"North what?" the second said. "I was born and raised in this town."

"Well, by God! the youth said. He looked about with a strained, battled gaze, as if he was trying to remember what it was he wanted to say or to do. He drew his sleeve across his sweating face. "Damn if I'm going to let a white woman—"

"You tell them, Jack," the drummer said. "By God if they—"

The screen door crashed open. A man stood in the floor, his feet apart and his heavy-set body poised easily. His white shirt was open at the throat; he wore a felt hat. His hot, bold glance swept the group. His name was McLendon. He had commanded troops at the front in France and had been decorated for valor?

"Well," he said, "are you going to sit there and let a black son rape a white woman on the streets of Jefferson?

Butch sprang up again. The silk of his shirt clung flat to his heavy shoulders. At each armpit was a dark halfmoon. I hat s what I been telling them! That's what I—"

"I lid it really happen? a third said. I his aint the first man scare she ever had, like Hawkshaw says. Wasn't there something about a man on the kitchen roof, watching her undress, about a year ago?

"What?" the client said. "What's that?" The barber had been slowly forcing him back into the chair; he arrested himself reclining, his head lifted, the barber still pressing him down.

McLendon whirled on the third speaker. "Happen? What the hell difference does it make? Are you going to let the black sons get away with it until one really does it?"

"That's what I'm telling them!" Butch shouted. He cursed, long and steady, pointless.

"Here, here," a fourth said. "Not so loud. Dont talk so loud."

"Sure," McLendon said; "no talking necessary at all. I've done my talking. Who's with me?" He poised on the balls of his feet, roving his gaze.

The barber held the drummer's face down, the razor poised. "Find out the facts first, boys. I know Willy Mayes. It wasn't him. Let's get the sheriff and do this thing right."

McLendon whirled upon him his furious, rigid face. The barber did not look away. They looked like men of different races. The other barbers had ceased also above their prone clients. "You mean to tell me," McLendon said, "that you'd take a nigger's word before a white woman's? Why, you damn niggerloving—"

The third speaker rose and grasped McLendon's arm; he too had been a soldier. "Now, now. Let's figure this thing out. Who knows anything about what really happened?"

"Figure out hell!" McLendon jerked his arm free. "All that're with me get up from there. The ones that aint—" He roved his gaze, dragging his three men rose. Thc drummer in the chair sat up. "Herr," he said, jerking at the doth about his neck; "get this rag off me. I'm with him. I dont live here, but by God, if our mothers and wives and sisters— He smeared the doth over his face and flung it to the floor. McLendon stood in the floor and cursed the others. Another rose and moved toward him. The remainder sat uncomfortable, not looking at one another, then one by one they rose and joined him.

The barber picked the doth from the floor. He began to fold it neatly.

"Boys, dont do that. Will Mayes never done it. I know."

"Come on," McLendon said. He whirled. From his hip pocket protruded the butt of a heavy automatic pistol. They went out. The screen door crashed behind them reverberant in the dead air.

The barber wiped the razor carefully and swiftly, and put it away, and ran to the rear, and took his hat from the wall. "I'll be back as soon as I can,' he said to the other barbers. "I cant let—" He went out, running. The two other barbers followed him to the door and caught it on the re-bound, leaning out and looking up the street after him. The air was flat and dead. It had a metallic taste at the base of the tongue.

"What can he do?" the first said. The second one was saying "Jees Christ, Jees Christ" under his breath. "I'd just as lief be Will Mayes as Hawk, if he gets McLendon riled." "Jees Christ, Jees Christ," the second whispered.

"You reckon he really done it to her?" the first said.

II

She was thirty-eight or thirty-nine. She lived in a small frame house with her invalid mother and a thin, sallow, unflagging aunt, where each morning between ten and eleven she would appear on the porch in a lace trimmed boudoir cap, to sit swinging in the porch swing until noon. After dinner she lay down for a while, until the afternoon began to cool. Then, in one of the three or four new voile dresses which she had each summer, she would go downtown to spend the afternoon in the stores with the other ladies, where they would handle the goods and haggle over the prices in cold, immediate voices, without any intention of buying.

She was of comfortable people—not the best in Jefferson, but good people enough—and she was still on the slender side of ordinary looking, with a bright, faintly haggard manner and dress. When she was young she had had a slender, nervous body and a sort of hard vivacity which had enabled her for a time to ride upon the crest of the town's social life as exemplified by the high school party and church social period of her contemporaries while still children enough to be unclassconscious.

She was the last to realize that she was losing ground; that those among whom she had been a little brighter and louder flame than any other were beginning to learn the pleasure of snobbery—male—and retaliation—female. That was when her face began to wear that bright, haggard look. She still carried it to parties on shadowy porticoes and summer lawns, like a mask or a flag, with that bafflement of furious repudiation of truth in her eyes. One evening at a party she heard a boy and two girls, -all schoolmates, talking. She never accepted another invitation.

She watched the girls with whom she had grown up as they married and got homes and children, but no man ever called on her steadily until the children of the other girls had been calling her "aunty" for several years, while their mothers told them in bright voices about how popular Aunt Minnie had been as a girl. Then the town began to see her driving on Sunday afternoons with the cashier in the bank. He was a widower of about forty—a high-colored man, smelling always faintly of the barber shop or of whisky. He owned the first automobile in town, a red runabout; Minnie had the first motoring bonnet and veil the town ever saw.[8] Then the town began to say: "Poor Minnie." But she is old enough to take care of herself," others said. That was when she began to ask her old schoolmates that their children call her "cousin" instead of "aunty."

It was twelve years now since she had been relegated into adultery by public opinion, and eight years since the cashier had gone to a Memphis bank, returning for one day each Christmas, which he spent at an annual bachelors' party at a hunting club on the river. From behind their curtains the neighbors would see the party pass, and during the over-the-way Christmas day visiting they would tell her about him, about how well he looked, and how they heard that he was prospering in the city, watching with bright, secret eyes her haggard, bright face. Usually by that hour there would be the scent of whisky on her breath. It was supplied her by a youth, a clerk at the soda fountain: "Sure; I buy it for the old gal. I reckon she's entitled to a little fun."

Her mother kept to her room altogether now. The gaunt aunt ran the house. Against that background Minnie's bright dresses, her idle and empty days, had a quality of furious unreality. She went out in the evenings only with women now, neighbors, to the moving pictures. Each afternoon she dressed in one of the new dresses and went downtown alone, where her young "cousins" were already strolling in the late afternoons with their delicate, silken heads and thin, awkward arms and conscious hips, clinging to one another or shrieking and giggling with paired boys in the soda fountain when she passed and went on along the serried store fronts, in the doors of which the sitting and lounging men did not even follow her with their eyes any more.

III

The Barber went swiftly up the street where the sparse lights, insect- swirled, glared in rigid and violent suspension in the lifeless air. The day had died in a pall of dust; above the darkened square, shrouded by the spent dust, the sky was as clear as the inside of a brass bell. Below the east was a rumor of the twice-waxed moon.

When he overtook them McLendon and three others were getting into a car parked in an alley. McLendon stooped his thick head, peering out beneath the top. “Changed your mind, did you?” he said. “Damn good thing; by God, tomorrow when this town hears about how you talked to night—”

“Now, now,” the other ex-soldier said. “Hawkshaw’s all right. Come on, Hawk; jump in.”

“Will Mayes never done it, boys,” the barber said. “If anybody done it. Why, you all know well as I do there aint any town where they got better niggers than us. And you know how a lady will kind of think things about men when there aint any reason to, and Miss Minnie anyway—”

“Sure, sure,” the soldier said. “We’re just going to talk to him a little; that’s all.”

“Talk hell!” Butch said. “When we’re through with the—”

“Shut up, for God’s sake!” the soldier said. “Do you want everybody in town—”

“Tell them, by God!” McLendon said. “Tell every one of the sons that’ll let a white woman—”

“Let’s go; let’s go: here’s the other car.” The second car slid squealing out of a cloud of dust at the alley mouth. McLendon started his car and took the lead. Dust lay like fog in the street. The street lights hung nimbused as in water. They drove on out of town.

A rutted lane turned at right angles. Dust hung above it too, and above all the land. The dark bulk of the ice plant, where the Negro Mayes was night watchman, rose against the sky. “Better stop here, hadn’t we?” the soldier said. McLendon did not reply. He hurled the car up and slammed to a stop, the headlights glaring on the blank wall.

“Listen here, boys,” the barber said; “if he’s here, dont that prove he never done it? Dont it? If it was him, he would run.

Dont you see he would?" The second car came up and stopped. McLendon got down; Butch sprang down beside him. "Listen, boys," the barber said.

"Cut the lights off!" McLendon said. The breathless dark rushed down. There was no sound in it save their lungs as they sought air in the parched dust in which for two months they had lived; then the diminishing crunch of McLendon's and Butch's feet, and a moment later McLendon's voice:

"Will! . . . Will!"

Below the east the wan hemorrhage of the moon increased. It heaved above the ridge, silvering the air, the dust, so that they seemed to breathe, live, in a bowl of molten lead. There was no sound of nightbird nor insect, no sound save their breathing and a faint ticking of contracting metal about the cars. Where their bodies touched one another they seemed to sweat dryly, for no more moisture came. "Christ!" a voice said; "let's get out of here."

But they didn't move until vague noises began to grow out of the darkness ahead; then they got out and waited tensely in the breathless dark. There was another sound: a blow, a hissing expulsion of breath and McLendon cursing in undertone. They stood a moment longer, then they ran forward. They ran in a stumbling clump, as though they were fleeing something. "Kill him, kill the son," a voice whispered. McLendon flung them back.

"Not here," he said. "Get him into the car." "Kill him, kill the black son!" the voice murmured. They dragged the Negro to the car. The barber had waited beside the car. He could feel himself sweating and he knew he was going to be sick at the stomach.

"What is it, captains?" the Negro said. "I aim done nothing. 'Fore God, Mr John." Someone produced handcuffs. They worked busily about the Negro as though he were a post, quiet, intent, getting in one another's way. He submitted to the handcuffs, looking swiftly and constantly from dim face to dim face. "Who's here, captains?" he said, leaning to peer into the faces until they could feel his breath and smell his sweaty reek. He spoke a name or two. "What you all say I done, Mr John?"

McLendon jerked the car door open. "Get in!" he said.

The Negro did not move. “What you all going to do with me, Mr John? I aint done nothing. White folks, captains, I aim done nothing: I swear ‘fore God.” He called another name.

“Get in!” McLendon said. He struck the Negro. The others expelled their breath in a dry hissing and struck him with random blows and he whirled and cursed them, and swept his manacled hands across their faces and slashed the barber upon the mouth, and the barber struck him also. “Get him in there,” McLendon said. They pushed at him. He ceased struggling and got in and sat quietly as the others took their places. He sat between the barber and the soldier, drawing his limbs in so as not to touch them, his eyes going swiftly and constantly from face to face. Butch clung to the running board. The car moved on. The barber nursed his mouth with his handkerchief.

“What’s the matter, Hawk?” the soldier said.

“Nothing,” the barber said. They regained the highroad and turned away from town. The second car dropped back out of the dust. They went on, gaining speed, the fmalfringe of houses dropped behind.

“Goddamn, he stinks!” the soldier said.

“We’ll fix that,” the drummer in front beside McLendon said. On the running board Butch cursed into the hot rush of air. The barber leaned suddenly forward and touched McLendon’s arm.

“Let me out, John,” he said.

“Jump out, niggerlover,” McLendon said without turning his head. He drove swiftly. Behind them the sourceless lights of the second car glared in the dust. Presently McLendon turned into a narrow road. It was rutted with disuse. It led back to an abandoned brick kiln—a series of reddish mounds and weed- and vine-choked vats without bottom. It had been used for pasture once, until one day the owner missed one of his mules. Although he prodded carefully in the vats with a long pole, he could not even find the bottom of them.

“John,” the barber said.

“Jump out, then,” McLendon said, hurling the car along the ruts. Beside the barber the Negro spoke: “Mr Henry.”

The barber sat forward. The narrow tunnel of the road rushed up and past. Their motion was like an extinct furnace blast: cooler, but utterly dead. The car bounded from rut to rut.

"Mr Henry," the Negro said.

The barber began to tug furiously at the door. "Look out, there!" the soldier said, but the barber had already kicked the door open and swung onto the running board. The soldier leaned across the Negro and grasped at him, but he had already jumped. The car went on without checking speed.

The impetus hurled him crashing through dust-sheathed weeds, into the ditch. Dust puffed about him, and in a thin, vicious crackling of sapless stems he lay choking and retching until the second car passed and died away. Then he rose and limped on until he reached the highroad and turned toward town, brushing at his clothes with his hands. The moon was higher, riding high and clear of the dust at last, and after a while the town began to glare beneath the dust. He went on, limping. Presently he heard cars and the glow of them grew in the dust behind him and he left the road and crouched again in the weeds until they passed. McLendon's car came last now. There were four people in it and Butch was not on the running board.

They went on; the dust swallowed them; the glare and the sound died away. The dust of them hung for a while, but soon the eternal dust absorbed it again. The barber climbed back onto the road and limped on toward town.

IV

As she dressed for supper on that Saturday evening, her own flesh felt 'ever. Her hands trembled among the hooks and eyes, and her eyes a feverish look, and her hair swirled crisp and crackling under the comb. While she was still dressing the friends called for her and sat while she donned her sheerest underthings and stockings and a new voile dress. 'Do you feel strong enough to go out?" they said, their eyes bright too, with a dark glitter. "When you have had time to get over the shock, you must tell us what happened. What he said and did; everything."

In the leafed darkness, as they walked toward the square, she began to breathe deeply, something like a swimmer preparing to dive, until she ceased trembling, the lorn of them walking slowly because of the terrible heat and out of solicit tide for her. But as they neared the square she began to tremble again, walking with hei head up, her hands clenched at her sides, their voices about her murmurous, also with that feverish, glittering, quality of their eyes.

They entered the square, she in the center of the group, fragile in her fresh dress. She was trembling worse. She walked slower and slower, as children eat ice cream, her head up and her eyes bright in the haggard banner of her face, passing the hotel and the coatless chummers in chaitn along the curb looking around at her: "That's the one: see? The one in pink in the middle." "Is that her? What did they do with the nigger? Did they—?""Sure. He's all right." "All right, is he?" "Sure. He went on a little-trip." Then the drug store, where even the young men lounging in the door-way tipped their hats and followed with their eyes the motion of her hips and legs when she passed.

They went on, passing the lifted hats of the gentlemen, the suddenly ceased voices, deferent, protective. Do you see? the friends said. Their voices sounded like long, hovering sighs of hissing exultation. " There's not a Negro on the square. Not one."

They reached the picture show. It was like a miniature fairyland with its lighted lobby and colored lithographs of life caught in its terrible and beautiful mutations.[12] Her lips began to tingle. In the dark, when the picture began, it would be all right; she could hold back the laughing so it would not waste away so fast and so soon. So she hurried on before the turning faces, the undertones of low astonishment, and they took their accustomed places where she could see the aisle against the silver glare and the young men and girls coming in two and two against it.

The lights flicked away; the screen glowed silver, and soon life began to unfold, beautiful and passionate and sad, while still the young men and girls entered, scented and sibilant in the half dark, their paired backs in silhouette delicate and sleek, their slim, quick bodies awkward, divinely young, while beyond them the silver dream accumulated, inevitably on and on. She began to laugh. In trying to suppress it, it made more noise than ever; heads began to turn. Still laughing, her friends raised her and led her out, and she stood at the curb, laughing on a high, sustained note, until the taxi came up and they helped her in.

They removed the pink voile and the sheer underthings and the stockings, and put her to bed, and cracked ice for her temples, and sent for the doctor. He was hard to locate, so they ministered to her with hushed ejaculations, renewing the ice and fanning her. While the ice was fresh and cold she stopped laughing and lay still for a time, moaning only a little. But soon the laughing welled again and her voice rose screaming.

"Shhhhhhhhhhh! Shhhhhhhhhhhhhhh!" they said, freshening the icepack, smoothing her hair, examining it for gray; "poor girl!" Then to one another: "Do you suppose anything really happened?" their eyes darkly aglitter, secret and passionate, "Shhhhhhhhhh! Poor girl! Poor Minnie!"

V

It was midnight when McLendon drove up to his neat new house. It was trim and fresh as a birdcage and almost as small, with its clean, green-and-white paint. He locked the car and mounted the porch and entered. His wife rose from a chair beside the reading lamp. McLendon stopped in the floor and stared at her until she looked down.

"Look at the clock," he said, lifting his arm, pointing. She stood before him, her face lowered, a magazine in her hands. Her face was pale, strained, and weary-looking. "Haven't I told you about sitting up like this, waiting to see when I come in?"

"John," she said. She laid the magazine down. Poised on the balls of his feet, he glared at her with his hot eyes, his sweating face.

"Didn't I tell you?" He went toward her. She looked up then. He caught her shoulder. She stood passive, looking at him.

"Don't John. I couldn't sleep . . . The heat; something. Please, John. You're hurting me."

"Didn't I tell you?" He released her and half struck, half flung her across the chair, and she lay there and watched him quietly as he left the room.

He went on through the house, ripping off his shirt, and on the dark, screened porch at the rear he stood and mopped his head and shoulders with the shirt flung it away. He took the pistol from his hip and laid it on the table beside the bed, and sat on the bed and removed his shoes, and rose and slipped his trousers off. He was sweating again already, and he stooped and hunted furiously for the shirt. At last he found it and wiped his body again, and, with his body pressed against the dusty screen, he stood panting. There was no movement, no sound, not even an insect. The dark world seemed to lie stricken beneath the cold moon and the lidless stars.

Word notes, annotation, etc.

Section I

Through the bloody September … the first said.

bloody September twilight – Twilight of the September evening was red as blood due to draught and dry weather. There was no rain for 62 days. The blood colour also suggests the impending death of the negro, Will Mayes.

It has gone like a fire in dry grass – The rumour of Will Mayes's supposed rape of Miss Minnie Cooper. The rumour spread rapidly in the town of Jefferson. The outside weather is dry and hot and the people became like dry grass and they have no patience to listen to logic and reason.

Vitiated – Darken, spoilt

Stale – Dry

Pomade – lord, smear, grease

Lotion – ointment, cream

Nigger – the word is used to mean the black African-American in America. But, in reality no black people like this word to reveal their racial identity.

Reckon – consider, calculate

Aint – am not; is not; are not.

Hulking – heavily built; big

A white woman's word before a nigger's? – This is the expression of racial hatred by the hulking youth in the barber shop. They cannot believe that anybody can prefer black man priority to a white woman especially in American South.

Yon dawn nigger lover – This is the manifestation of hatred and anger towards the barber, Hawkshaw, who repeatedly supported in favour of the nigger i.e. Will Mayes.

Poised – self-assured
Dunn – Damned
Stubborn – obstinate

You better go back North – There was American Civil War from 1861-1865 on the issue of slavery. The North American States wanted to demolish slavery from America while the Southern Confederacy supported the continuance of Slavery System. Even after the abolition of Slavery, the Southern States continued to show their hatred and racial discrimination to the black people. So when Hawkshaw again and again was supporting Will Mayes, one youth told him angrily to go to North where black people get freedom and sympathy.

Strained – drawn
Baffled – surprised

Decorated for valor – Here the reference is to the American involvement in the first World War from 1914 to 1918. McLendon led a troop in France and he was rewarded for his bravery in the battlefield.

Reclining – Relaxing; leaning back
Whirled – Rotated; went round
Roving – wandering; drifting
Sheriff – Deputy; Officer of the law
Smeared – marked; tarnished
Protruded – stood out; came through
Reverberant – Resounding; resonant

Jees Christ – Jesus Christ; the second barber again and again utters this word as if he felt the impending fate of Will Mayes and so he remembers the name of the Lord to save all and give peace.

Section II

Un-flagging – Tireless; persistent
Porch – vestibule; entry
Boudoir cap – A cap made of light fabric such as Muslin etc.
Voile – A fine, soft fabric
Haggle – Barter, negotiate
Haggard – Tired; unwell

Slender – slim; lean
Vivacity – Liveliness; scintillation
Exemplified – Demonstrated, illustrated
Unclassconscious – class prejudice; class identity
Snobbery – Affectation
Retaliation – Revenge; vengeance
Porticoes – veranda; porch
Repudiation – Refuse; reject
Runabout – car; open wagon
Relegated – Downgraded; lowered
Gaunt – skin and bones; haggard

Section III

Insect-swirled – whirled by insects
Pau of dust – cloud of dust
Slid – glide; slip
Squealing – screaming
Nimbused – furnished with nimbus
Rutted – corrugated; uneven
Hurled – thrown; tossed
Parched – Dried

Wan hemorrhage of the moon – This is a symbolic reference that Will Mayes is going to be murdered soon.

Clump – cluster; group

Handcuffs – manacles; fetters; symbol of black slavery to white people of America

Reek – stink; smell
Mounds – Heap; pile
Kiln – furnace; fire
Vats – Tubs; Tanks
Tug – Pull
Impetus – Momentum
Dust-sheathed – Embowered with dust
Vicious – Brutal; dangerous

Butch was not on the running board – The line symbolically mean that the action of lynching is completed and Butch, on their return to town, sat inside the car in a seat in which Will Mayes sat when the car was moving towards the kiln.

limped – Hawkshaw jumped from the running car and as result was injured and so he was limping to return to the town.

Section IV

Her own flesh felt like fever – while on the ere of Will Mayes's murder, Minnie and her friends were going to the Sauane in town, Minnie was feeling feverish probably as a result of nervous breakdown hearing the news of Mayes's murder.

Swirled – whirled; spiraled

Crisp – crunchy

Crackling – Hissing, sizzling

Their eyes bright, too – Here the friends of Miss Minnie Cooper are referred. They were actually anxious to know about Minnie's incident with that black man and they were interested in more gossip.

Ceased – stopped

Solicitude – concern; care

Clenched – clasped; gripped

Fragile – Breakable

He went on a little trip – This line shows the casual attitude of the white people towards black Mayes. The negro died and they commented with a bantering tone that he went on a little trip.

Deferent – dissimilar

Exultation – Jubilation

Miniature – small

Lithographs – Lithography is a printing technology in which the image to be printed is rendered on a flat surface, as on a sheet zinc or aluminium. A lithograph is a print produced by lithography.

Tingle – prickle; sling

Aisle – passage; corridor

Sibilant – swoosh; wheeze

Silhouette – shape; figure

She began to laugh – This is the effect of poetic justice. On the eve of Will Mayes's killing, Minnie and her friends went to see a cinema. But as soon as the cinema began, she began to laugh loudly probably due to her nervous breakdown.

ejaculations – Emission; discharge

poor girl – Minnie's friends commented about her when she again and again lost her nerves. They noticed a number of grey hair on her head and expressed their comic sympathy for her who still could not marry at all.

Section V

Birdcage – McLeadon's house was a small as a birdcage, without enough fresh air.

Her face was pale – When McLeadon extended the room and looked at his wife with his angry face, his face became pale. Here "pale face" reminds the readers of McLeadon's angry face.

Glared – looked fixedly

I couldn't sleep…the heat – McLeadon's wife could not sleep due to excessive heat. It is symbolic that she was feeling the same heat as her husband's inner heat after the lynching.

Hunted furiously for the shirt – McLeadon felt restless and he could not bear the unbearable heat and excessive sweating. So he was searching for the shirt furiously.

Cold moon and the lidless stars – The reference of the cold moon is metaphoric as everything is done. Will Mayes was lynched and everything seems to be cool. Lidless stars has a reference of the hall in D.G. Ressetti's poem "Inclusiveness" the last two lines of which are as follows:

"And may be stamped, a memory all in vain/upon the sight of lidless eyes in Hell."

Literally, McLeadon is living in a condition like hell after he committed the crime of murdering Will Mayes.

CRITICAL SUMMARY OF 'DRY SEPTEMBER'

"'Dry September' is one of Faulkner's best known and most characteristic stories. Even among readers who otherwise know little of Faulkner's work, many seem to know "that storm where the black guy rapes the Ole white woman and gets lynched". It did not happen this way, of course, but that is frequently how the tale is remembered—perhaps readers are more taken by the story's rumours and sensationalism than they would like to admit". [John K. Crane]

There are five parts in the story. Section one, three and five deal with the rumour and mob murder of Will Mayes, the Negro accused of raping Minnie Cooper, an aging spinster, and the second and fourth sections deals with Minnie as she attempts to recapture a small position of her exciting but now dead past.

The story starts with an unnatural state of nature i.e. it has not rained for 62 days and in that condition a rumour spread like fire in dry grass "through the bloody September twilight" that Miss Minnie Cooper, a local white spinster, aged between 38 or 39, has been raped by a negro man named Will Mayes. Furious white youths gathered in the local barber's shop in Jefferson. They felt insulted that a black nigger can commit such a sexual crime against a white woman. It is a matter of pride and honour to them. And also a matter of revenge. But the owner of the barber's shop, Stenry Hawkshaw expresses his doubt about the rumous and again and again he repeats that he knows Will Mayes well and asserts that he cannot commit such a crime against the white lady Minnie Cooper. The white youths present in his shop accuse him of being a "nigger lover". In spite of all that Hawkshaw says that likely nothing happened at all. One of the white youths angrily tells him to "go back to North"and John McLeadon, an army officer angrily asks him, "are you going to let a black son rape a white woman on the streets of Jefferson?" Hawkshaw tried to resist them from giving death penalty to that black Negro, but in vein. Under the leadership of John McLeadon, all the white youth go in search of that supposed black victim and Hawkshaw follows them with the faint hope that he might be able to save Mayes from their cruel hands. He rushes after them with a thought—"I can't let". The two other barbers discuss among themselves if Will Mayes really did anything to Miss Minnie Cooper.

Minnie Cooper, a 38 or 39 years old lady, lives in a small house with her old mother and aunt. Her life is bound by a uniform routine:

getting up at 10:00 a.m., swinging on her porch in the morning; napping; dressing up and going downtown with her friends. She was invited in social events for sometimes at her early youths; but her friends became aware about class differences and later she was neglected to be invited. All her friends were married and settled down in life. But Minnie remained a spinster permanently. Once she began to ride around the town with the cashier of bank. The man had the first automobile in Jefferson and he was a widower. People became curious about their affair. But the bank cashier got a new job at Memphis and left Jefferson. Once in a year on the Christmas days he used to come to Jefferson, but he made party with his friends and never invited Minnie. Miss Minnie Cooper started to drink whisky that was brought to her by a boy who took pity on her and thought that "she's entitled to a little fun".

The day is almost dark with a veil of dust. Henry Hawkshaw, the so-called nigger-lover, joins the group of McLeadon who were driving out to the ice factory to catch Will Mayes. Hawkshaw again tries to explain that Will Mayes was innocent; otherwise he would run away. But no one is ready to listen to him. The angry white youths called Will Mayes, handcuffed him, took him to the car and sped up on the dusty roads. Hawkshaw sat beside Will Mayes but he thought of leaving the killer party. He requested McLeadon to stop the car but McLeadon ordered him to jump from the speeding car. Hawkshaw did so and he fell into a ditch. He was cloked and was retching in the dry grass. He began to move towards home. After a while, McLeadon's car passed from the other direction. This time he noticed that Will Mayes was not there inside the car. There was moon in the sky but nothing was clearly visible as the dust adhered to everything.

On the day of Will Mayes' abduction and mob lynching, Minnie Cooper feels feverish and nervous. She feels trembling. She wants to go out with her friends and they help her to prepare for the outing. Her friends want to know more about Will Mayes. Minnie remains silent and they all reach to the Square. The evening heat was unbearable and Minnie feels uneasy and starts to trembling again. She can't control herself. They return home and the people in the street look at her with curiosity. There was a new rumour among the people that Will Mayes "Went to a little trip". There were no black people on the Square that evening. That was really remarkable. Minnie and her friends enter into a movie with a hope that Minnie will calm down and control herself. But there inside the cinema hall a fit of laughter arises and she cannot control it. She laughed so loudly that her friends came out of the hall and brought her in a taxi. They rub ice on her forehead and call the doctor. But Minnie's fit of laughter does not stop at all.

After committing the death settlement of Will Mayes, McLeadon returns to his house at midnight. He got furious to see his wife awake till then. She scolds his wife waiting for him. His wife replied that she was not waiting for him, but she could not sleep for excessive heat. But McLeadon got furious again and grabs her shoulder and hurts her. He strikes her and left her crumpled across the chair and he himself left the room. He went to the porch and undress himself. He tries to wipe his excessive sweat from his face and whole body. But he seats again. He stands at the dusty screen and pants heavily in the silent night under the lidless stars.

CRITICAL ANALYSIS OF 'DRY SEPTEMBER'

"Dry September" is undoubtedly Faulkner's most celebrated short story. The readers who do not know the title of this story seem to know "the story where black negro rapes the white lady and get lynched". This is the way how this story is remembered. According to William Van O'Connor, Dry September is "a story of the wretchedness, the sadism, and the shame of a man who has helped to lynch a Negro". Another interpretation of the story by John Vicky is scapegoat and ritual theory. And there is other group of people who believe in Farenheit reading of the story who believe that heat is deterministically responsible for most of the vile incidents that occur in the story.

Faulkner wrote the story in lazy and sent it in 1930 to the *American Mercury* with the original title "Drouth". But unfortunately the story was rejected by the 'American Mercury'. Faulkner revised the story, mainly the first two sections, changed the title from 'Drouth' to "Dry September" and it seems that

Faulkner switched the emphasis from the white woman to weather. He also brought the character of McLendon as the leader of the mob. However, this time he sent the story to 'Scribner's' and it was accepted published in January, 1931.

The beginning line of the story sets the mood of the whole story: "Bloody September twilight, aftermath of sixty-two rainless days. It is the weather then plays a vital role in the story, at least in the month of the characters. One of the character in the story says, "It is this down weather… It's enough to make a man do anything". The indication is hence the supposed rape of Miss Minnie Cooper by the black man, Will Mayes. The air is dead, and McLendon has "a metallic taste at the base of the tongue". Dust plays a vital role in the story. "Dust lay fog in the street. The street lights hung, nimbused as in water". All these things adds to the tone and mood of the story. Faulkner subtly but unmistaken tries to show that the motivation of all malpractices lies elsewhere.

Dry September also relates to human existence in this earth in terms of seasonal cycle. Spring is the season of youthful vigour and new life; summer is the season of early maturity and growing; Autumn means middle age and harvest; winter relates to old age and frozen nature. September denotes both late summer and early autumn. But the term "Dry September" indicates little growth and poor harvest. This is the period of frustration and despair to the farmers. However, the term 'dry September' is mentioned a dozen of times in the story. But in the second and fourth sections of the story, this dryness is mentioned once each and that also centers a Minnie. It means dry middle age and internal heat that compels her to accuse Will Mayes. The other heat description are given in remaining three sections i.e. section one, three and five and those heat descriptions focus on Jack McLendon whose life and activities are in a figurative dry September, indeed. And this figurative dry September motivated both Minnie and McLendon; the former the accuse Will Mayes, and the latter to kill him.

"Dry September" is a problematic story to elucidate to the readers. The story deals with sympathy and antipathy quite simultaneously. It is quite difficult to identify the male factor in the story. Sometimes it seems that Miss Minnie Cooper is **the** villain; But at the same time it is still possible to see McLendon as a villain. The readers may get baffled if they read the story in terms of individual psychology, with the emphasis on female sex and hysterical attitude; on the other hand, in terms of social psychology, and a particular class of American society as described by Faulkner at a particular time. The psycho-sexual rumour of racial bigotry is openly demonstrated in the story. Though Faulkner's analysis is of multi-directed, there is one person in the story who can talk over right or wrong and almost force people to follow him. The white youths are excited to do something but actually they do not know what really happened. They even don't bother to know the truth. They are angry because they are "attacked, insulted, frightened" by the other "race". This blind racism leads to dangerous casualties—the death of a black man, Will Mayes who even does not know what his fault is.

Amid all these heat, burn and humdrum, there is only one person who acts as a conscience to lost humanity. He is Hawkshaw, the barber who always tries to persuade all the white youths including McLendon that Will Mayes cannot do such a base act as raping Miss Minnie Cooper. He knows both Will Mayes and Minnie Cooper, who is around 40 and has never been married. He tries to implore all: "I leave it to you fellows if then ladies that get old without getting married don't have notions that a man can't …". All the people in barber shop admit that the rumour of Will Mayes is "not the first man scare she ever had…". So Hawkshaw tries to establish the fact that Minnie's words should not be taken as true. But his words have no effect on the listeners. They are not in a position to believe that a white woman could be lying. It is a fact that even if Minnie has become a laughing-stock for these youths, they are eager to "defend here" and go to the point of killing the nigger. This is a clear indication of male bigotry in addition to racism. All the white youth including their leader McLendon bully Hawkshaw as the "nigger-lover". He angrily declares: "I'd just as life be Will Mayes as Hawk, if he gets McLendon riled". So all the white youths join McLendon and leave with him in search of the victim, Will Mayes. Hawkshaw, the conscience of humanity, also joins with the party with a faint hope if he could save Will

Mayes but in vain. When he walks to join them, the description of drought, dust and death prevails: "The day had died in a pale of dust; above the darkened Square, shrouded by the spent dust; the sky was as clear as the inside of a brass bell. Below the east was a rumour of twice-waxed moon". The line "Below the east the wan hemorrhage of the moon increased" suggest the pending death of an innocent man. But surely enough, there is no direct reference of that lynching show. Faulkner craftily avoided that violent action from his narrative. Only the reference is there. Will Mayes was not inside the car when the team of angry white youths were returning from the kiln. There is only reference of bottomless rats that is enough to indicate about the destiny of Will Mayes. On that evening when Minnie and her friends went to the movie, people were talking about the incident. Some people in the town were asking the question: "What did they do with the nigger? Did they…?" The public opinion was ambiguous but clear: "Sure, he is alright", "Sure, he went on a little trip". Such was a public mention of Jefferson after the killing of a black man. Hawkshaw's attempts could not save him either.

The instincts of violence harboured by McLendon and his comrades is not restricted in themselves, but such instincts also underlie the behaviour of the women who accompany Minnie. In the past, Minnie was more popular than them, and now they sensed a "pleasure of retaliation", they try to focus the negative character of Minnie as an unmarried woman and they help her to enter into her personal hell. Here in this story the 'hell' is the fruit of a long and articulate chain where cruelty and selfishness nourishes an infinite, long process. When Hawkshaw leaves his shop, one of the barbers murmurs—"Jees Christ, Jees Christ". Will Mayes is the only character in the story who reminds the readers the figure of Jesus Christ, both of them are innocent and both of them were watchmen—Will Mayes of the ice plant, Jesus Christ of the oppressed humanity. Only difference is that, Jesus Christ pardoned his killers, while Will Mayes cursed them.

SOME ESSAYS ON "DRY SEPTEMBER"

(a) Comment on the Title of the story "DRY SEPTEMBER"

"Dry September" was originally entitled as "Drouth" and sent to *American Mercury* but it was rejected to be published in 1930. Faulkner then revised and rewrote the story and sent the story with the title "Dry September" to another magazine *Scribner's* in 1931 and it got published and caught the attention of the readers. The host, dry September weather which gave rise to the dust is now causing to breathe unusually deep.

"The bloody September twilight, aftermath of sixty-two rainless days" sets the mood of the story from the beginning. The dum weather of dry September can make a man do anything. McLendon's face sweats throughout the story and at the end he sits naked on his bed wiping himself dry with his T-shirt. The air outside was almost dead and McLendon has a metallic taste at the base of his tongue. Dust lay like fog in the street. The street light hung nimbused as in water.

"Dry September" also refers to a very common mythical understanding of human existence. September is a period of poor harvest and little growth. It is also a season of frustration and despair. So in the title of the story, the theme and mood of the story is reflected perfectly. The story deals with aridity, sweaty and stale air. The air gets saturated with dust and the dark setting resembles the underworld or inferno. Hell is not a place but a state of mind of those who feel the desperation of being alienated from God. Hell is the spiritual and psychological punishment experienced by individuals who lives in the state of alienation by committing a sin which is nothing but "spiritual death". According to Edwards, "Spiritual death" entered into the word on the eve of fall i.e. Autumn, that occurs in September and it is a condition of Spiritual bankruptcy deriving from the loss of unification with the God. And this State of Spiritual death is eternal; it remains even after physical death unless the divine power saves one. In the story there are spiritual death of Minnie Cooper as well as McLendon. So, in course of the story, we find that, they feel "dryness" in their inner self—Minnie Cooper being psychologically unstable and here nerves being out of control and McLendon being extreme anger and feeling excessive heat and sweating continuously. They are, in fact, separated from their own race and their surrounding world. Minnie Cooper's separation and desperation produce a self-destructive inner-conflict in her. On the other hand, McLendon's separation and desperation produce a reverse effect. He wants to destroy the external world and in both their cases, they corrupt their mind. Minnie Cooper is corrupted because she accuses a black man of sexual violence, but probably that victim is totally unaware of the fact. McLendon is corrupted because he makes Will Mayes as his instrument to fulfill his sadistic attitude. Both of them feel the same infernal sceneries. As for McLendon, in the last part of the story, he contemplates in solitude the dark and silent world extending beyond the porch of his house which appears to him "stricken beneath the cold moon and the lidless stars".

McLendon has committed a sin to humanity. As result of that he cannot demonstrate love to the members of his family. It is evident from his behaviour that the possibility of conciliation with himself and other people in the family is totally absent from his life. He turns to sadistic violence as a means of asserting his existence because this is the only way he knows to find liberation from insurmountable desperation.

The excessive heat which dominates the story "Dry September" makes people aggressive and that heat is an important symbolic element in the story. One client in the barber shop comments, "It's this dum weather. Its enough to make a man do anything". Heat in the dry September may be defined as the manifestations of destiny inside and outside of human beings. It works as a stimulus in them. This excessive heat suppresses some characters in the story while some feel excited especially those who commit the violence of lynching innocent Will Mayes. Even Hawkshaw cannot avoid the course of heat effect. When Will Mayes being panic-stricken hits Hawkshaw by mistake. Hawkshaw cannot control himself and he returns the same hit to that helpless victim who he repeatedly wanted to save from the hands of the tormentors. But later Hawkshaw controls his anger but McLendon and his angry troops remain overwhelming and the "dry September" guide their actions.

In the story, Faulkner again and again mentions the motif of heat. In section 1, the story begins with the description of dry and hot weather: "Through the bloody September twilight, aftermath of sixty-two rainless days, it had gone like a fire in dry grass". And in section 5, wife of McLendon says: "Don't, John. I couldn't sleep ... the heat; something. Please, John. You're hurting me". The transfer of external heat into internal attitude of McLendon is quite clear here. Through this hot weather of September, the author wants to show that the whole world is in with immortality, racism and prejudice. There is no hope to them at all. Faulkner again and again repeats the word "dust"which stands for wickedness, corruption and mercilessness. And the title of the story "Dry September"may be interpreted as both appropriate and symbolic.

(b) Dust and Dryness as a Catalyst Theme in Faulkner's "DRY SEPTEMBER"

The weather plays a vital role in the short story "Dry September". And there is ever-present dust that encloses everything in the story. The dust is probably used to cover the guilt and crime which none of the characters can escape. But particularly speaking, dust stands for the whole perverted attitude of the Southern America. No one can get away from the dust effect. Even Hawkshaw cannot get away from it and is swept away by the crowd. The word 'dust' is used 15 times in the fourth section of the story and all the readers are choxed by the extremely intense presence of the dust in everywhere. Whenever someone takes a breath, it fills the mouth. Faulkner used the word 'dust' again and again in the story:

"Day lay like tog in the street".

"Dust hung above it too, and above all the land".

"There was no sound in it saver their lungs as they sought air in the parched dust in which for two months they had lived".

Even the moon is not escaped by dust.

"Below the east the wan hemorrhage of the moon increased. It heaved above the rise, silvering the air, the dust, so that they seemed to breathe, live, in a bowl of matter lead".

When Hawkshaw realized the impossibility of saving the black man, he jumps from the car. He is covered with dust beside the road.

"The impetus hurled him crashing through the dust-Sheathed Weeds, into the ditch. Dust puffed around the eyes of Hawkshaw 'the town began to glare beneath the dust". And when the actual murder of Will takes place, he engulfs the speeding cars. Hawkshaw stood still and the lights of the cars 'grew in the dust' passed him, and returned to the dust. At the end of section 4 the readers see how the dust than men had raised will simply be absorbed by the ever-present dust.

On the other hand, the unnatural hot weather evokes an infernal atmosphere in the story and plays an important role in the development of the plot. The weather affects the temper of the towns people to their "easily fanned frustrations". They are not likely to act and behave normally. People in the barber shop are inflamed with rage and they have a caustic argument over the rumour. At that point, someone blames the weather: "It is the dum weather; it's enough to make a man do anything. Even to her". They discuss that the rumour spread like "a fire in dry grass". The bloody colour of twilight after a long drought foreshadows the impending violence and death that will occur in the life of Will Mayes.

"Through the bloody September twilight, aftermath of sixty-two rainless days, it had gone like a fire in dry grass—the rumour, the storm, whatever it was. Something about Miss Minnie Cooper and a Negro. Attacked, insulted, frightened".

"Dry September" also suggests the dryness of inner soul of the characters in the story. They are spiritually dry, like the solo speaker in the wasteland. Minnie Cooper is an aged lady of 38 or 39. It is here internal heat and dry middle age which motivate her to accuse the innocent Will Mayes with a stronger motif. Another character John McLendon also suffers from the same internal heat of dryness. With this excessive heat, his conscience and humanity is dried up. And with the influence of that excessive heat, he led the mob to kill the innocent man. The narrator of the story mentions the sweat on the characters several times. McLendon and Butch utter the word "heat" several times while they speak. Faulkner tries to unite heat, hell and sweat in the activities of the mob. The hell is not a particular place in the universe but a state of mind that make a human being to be suffered. So after the death of Mayer, Minnie Cooper suffer mental instability and McLendon suffers excessive heat and sweat at his home. He sweats profusely. If the blood and decay throughout the lead is symbolic of the death of Mayes; sweat is the excitement McLendon. No matter how much McLendon mops up his sweats, it comes back more. McLendon sweats more and more. But in spite of that, he doesn't cool off; his hate and anger is not over and as a result of it, the sweating continues. Sweat links like McLendon and dry air. Dry September is a passionate story that opens the eyes of the society in relation to weather and human beings.

(c) Racial Conflict: A Major Theme in the Story

Racial conflict and racial hatred are the major themes in Faulkner's short story—"Dry September". The incident of Will Mayes's abduction and lynching in the hands of an intoxicated white mob shows a critical point of view of racial relations between the white and the flock in the American South during 1920s. The situation highlights in the fact that white men are free to commit violent acts without fears of reprisal but the black men were criminalized without any valid reasons. Though Will Mayes is depicted as a submissive and innocent character, the racial hatred by the white people towards the flock turns to touch its zenith.

As the story starts, the white people gather in the local saloon of Jefferson. The rumour of Will Mayes's attempt to rape Minnie Cooper spread like a wild fire and the clients in the barber discuss on that topic. They even don't know Minnie Cooper, the white lady of about 40, but they give their support and sympathy to her. On the other hand, they clearly do not see Will Mayes as their equal. They even don't think that Will is a human being. They even don't call him by name. Rather they call him as "black son" or "nigger" and disgorge their despise to the flock community. It is only Hawkshaw, the white barber, who show respect and deep concern to Will Mayes. Hawkshaw stands out as a rational character in the story. His defense of Will Mayes is deeply established in his strong belief that Will is a "good nigger". He tries to advocate for Mayes who was a man of middle age; a thin, sand-coloured man with a mild face and who was his shaving client. He strongly said, "I know Will Mayes. He's a good nigger. And I know Miss Minnie Cooper too". But Hawkshaw's story is never heard and his argument goes in vain. Rather he is threatened by the white youths to be a "nigger lover" and he is advised to go to the North. Because, according to them there is no place in South, although he was born and brought up in South.

Now, the word "nigger" itself is a shameful term for the black people of America. This word has a long, violent history in the North American context. This word is used mainly as a racial, ethnic shun against African-American people who, in fact, do not like the word. According to Longston Huges, the great American poet, the word "nigger" is "used rightly or wrongly, ironically or seriously, of necessity for the sake of realism, or impishly for the sake of comedy, it doesn't matter". Negroes do not like it in any book or play whatsoever, be the book or play ever so sympathetic in its treatment of the basic problems of the race. Even though the book or play is written by a negros, they still do not like it. The word nigger, you see, sums up for us who are coloured all the bitter years of insult and struggle in America."

When the white men abduct Will Mayes, he attempts to remain as submissive as possible during his abduction. He politely asks that abductors what was happening and he calls them as "captains", "Mr. John" and "Mr. Henry". It is the time of getting him into the car when he struggle against them but at that time, too, he tries to "drawing his limbs in so as not to touch" the white men. He tries to defend himself, "I ain't done nothing. White folks, captains, I ain't done nothing: I swear 'fore God". But his appeal is meaningless to the heartless white mob. They took him to be guilty and took him to the kiln for lynching.

The mob expressing their anger and showed their racial hatred before killing Will Mayes. They attacked him both physically and verbally. Some of the white people wanted to kill him in the ice factory where Will worked. They were shouting, "Kill him! Kill the black son!" They put him into the car and strike him "with random blows". Their aim was to satisfy their own desire to inflict violence. They also handcuffed him although he remained submissive all the time. The handcuff is a symbol of flock slaves in shackles as they were brought work or to be killed by their white masters. This image strongly establish the fact that a black man can never be free within a deeply racist society like American South.

At the end of the story, when Cooper went to visit the Square in the town, people talk about her and Will Mayes:

"That's the one: See? The one in pink in the middle."

"Is that her? What did they do with the nigger? Did they?"

"Sure. He's all right".

"All right, is he?"

"Sure. He went on a little trip."

On the other hand, the friends who accompanied Minnie Cooper in the town, express their astonishment that there was no black men in the town:

"Do you see?" the friends said.

"There's not a Negro on the Square. Not one".

All these reactions by the common white people of Jefferson show their attitude towards the blacks. It is their indifference and prejudice for the black community that even after the death of Will Mayes, they can casually utter that "He went on a little trip.".

(d) Narrative Technique in "DRY SEPTEMBER"

William Faulkner's short story "Dry September" is narrated by a third person narrator who is reliable to the readers because he describes the incidents as they happen in the surrounding. The narration goes uninterrupted and the story is not fragmented as we find in Faulkner's other stories. The narrator conveys the facts of the story. He only recounts the characters' activities but does not interrupt them or make no judgments.

Faulkner wrote the story first with the little "Drouth" and sent the manuscript to the American magazine; but unfortunately the manuscript could not attract the attention of the editor and it was summarily rejected. Then he revised the manuscript in its plot and tone. The first two sections of the story were transposed and the description of the dry September weather came first and Minnie's part came in the section. And the story started with "the bloody September twilight, aftermath of sixty-two rainless days", and then follows the rumour of sexual harassment of the short story "Dry September", like Faulkner's other writings, demonstrate distinctive narrative technique. The use of metaphorical words like "rumour", "blood twilight" and "dust" have their functions with the theme and tone of the story. There is a relationship between the character and narration. The readers can assume that when McLendon and his white comrades drive the car for lynching Will Mayes, Minni Cooper may walk through the Square and was on the condition of losing her mind in the picture show. Faulkner's craft is there to create her character in the story. She is always on her way for places where men are. The places like high school party, church where young Minnie catches men's eyes, Serried stores fronts, in the doors of which sit men and the Square where she walks slowly in here illness. In diachronic relation, Minnie Cooper moves towards her definite direction for pursuing feminine charm or saving her dignity as a woman. Here lies the mastery of Faulkner as a narrative designer.

The structural manouvre of "Dry September" is so deliberate and clear that it seems to be natural and inescapable. Moreover, symbols, parallels and literary juxtaposition of elements are all maintained with dexterity. It is probable that the inspiration for the story was very strong to the author. But the narrative technique of the story was Faulkner's own original imagination. The dry weather lasted for 62 days and it seems that this dry weather has created an unrest among the people of Jefferson. Therefore, as soon as the rumour reaches the barber shop, it spreads like a fie in the dry grass. No one was intended to know "exactly what happened", but in spite of that they feel "attacked, insulted and frightened". They take the rumour as true and strongly believe that a white woman like Minnie cannot lie though they have no clear idea about Minnie's character. They emotionally express their racial prejudices and their highest conviction is that Will Mayes is a nigger, hence he is inferior and so they take "a white woman's words before a nigger's". The psycho-sexual point of racial discrimination is abundantly shown in the text, although Faulkner has multi-directional analysis and viewpoint. It is needless to explain when someone says, "This darn weather" can make anybody do anything.

Faulkner's narrative technique works perfectly well. Although the story is rigidly controlled, the execution of its master plan is hardly noticeable. The first two parts of the story are delineated from a diversity of perspectives. The third person narrator is in total control of his narrative. Though the narrator is not noticeable, he shifts from one speaker to another easily in the barber shop. The narrator also narrates the story of Minnie Cooper briefly so that the readers can make an idea about Minnie of their own. This treatment to Minnie evokes pity and compassion for her. It is evident that the narrator bears a sympathy for Minnie and has a stern criticism for the society and system that undermine others. His manner of narration is free and the readers are allowed to emulate the events that take place in the story one after another. Thus, Faulkner creates a chain of events and the technique allows him to avoid a direct description of a murder. The readers get a hint of that incident when Hawkshaw jumps from the moving car and McLendon does not care to stop the car. Moreover, allusion and metaphors give the readers a clear indication of Mayes's fate. The metaphors suggest that the heat and dry weather also apply to human beings and their relationships. There is also interrelation among climate, landscape and social conditions and terror and death that follow thereafter.

Faulkner's dexterity lies in letting the most violent action take place away from the direct narrative. Rather realism and rich imagery evoke a feeling of horror beyond doubt: "The moon was higher, riding high and clear of the dust at last, and after a while the town began the dust. He went on, limping. Presently he heard cars and the glow of them grew in the dust behind him and he left the road and crouched again in the weeds until they passed.

They went on; the dust swallowed them; the glare and the sound died away. The dust of them hung for a while, but soon the eternal dust absorbed it again. The barber climbed back onto the road and limped on toward home."

So, from the beginning to the end of the story, the readers react to the recurrent uses of images. 'Dust' is everywhere in the story and it plays an important role as a part of the dry, dark and lifeless social conditions. The word 'dust' gives the language a magical and engrossing force so that the readers can feel the basis of sound and rhythm, as much as on the basis of paradigmatic composition.

(e) Character of Minnie Cooper

Miss Minnie Cooper is an unmarried white lady of almost 40. Though she was attractive as a young girl, but she was passed over by the boys in town in favour of women with a higher social status. She may or may not have been sexually assaulted by a negro, Will Mayes. There is rumour only, but no proof was available that anything happened between the two—Minnie and Will Mayes. Some people of Jefferson even don't believe the rumour because they heard such type of 'man-scare' story of Minnie before. In fact, Miss Minnie has been virtually abandoned the people of her neighbourhood due to her low class and absence of a husband. Once she made dating with a widower, a bank cashier who had the first four wheeler in Jefferson, but that affair brought to her only rumour about her character. Moreover, that bank cashier later went to Memphis with a transfer but he did not care to take Minnie there. So, Minnie has to settle with her aging mother and an aunt who looks after their household. Minnie began to drink whiskey which is brought by a boy who used to say that "she's entitled to a little fun". When she accused Will Mayes of being the culprit to rape her, there was no true base on the accusation but it was a fact that she became the centre of attraction in town and most probably she wanted to become point of talk of the town in that way.

On the day of Will Mayes's being mob lynched, Minnie Cooper prepares to go out with her friends who were more interested in gossip with Mayes. They asked: "What he did and said, everything." Minnie replied nothing but began to trembling. But her friends were interested only in the gossip, not in her physical or psychological condition. Minnie's nervous breakdown and trembling may be due to two factors: If the rumour was true, she might be feeling a trauma of sexual violence by Mayes; and, if the rumour was false, she might have felt the biting of the conscience in her mind.

However, the news of the murder of Will Mayes spread all over the town. As Minnie and her friends walk down the street in the evening, Minnie is at the centre of the group, and she has to breathe deeply to control her nervous breakdown. People of the town look at their group, specially Minnie and they discuss about the rumour. People speak about Will Mayes that he "went on a little trip". They also speak about the fact that there was no black man on the Square that day. The lack of black men on the Square and in the town suggests that John McLendon's plan to scare the black people worked successfully.

Minnie and her friends then enters a movie theatre. They hope that there Minnie will be able to calm down her nerves. But more interestingly, she began to laugh loudly and this fit of laughter made her again the focus of attraction to all. It is not clear whether her fit of laughter is due to trauma or another plan to grab the attraction. Whatever else, her friends enjoy the situation in the pretense of helping her and they are more interested in partaking to gossip.

Minnie's friends bring her home in a cab. They fan her and rub ice on her forehead. This keeps her cool and stops the laughter-fit; but due to excessive heat, the effect of ice does not work for long. As soon as the ice melts, Minnie's fit of laughter returns. The heat of dry September makes Minnie insane. The dust in her inner mind stirs her entire physical and psychological state.

(f) Character of John McLendon

We get a clear picture of McLendon when he enters into the barber's shop. Faulkner describes:

"The screen door crashed open. A man stood in the floor, his feet apart and his heavy-set body poised easily. His white shirt was open at the throat; he wore a felt hat. His hot, bold glance swept the group. His name was McLendon. He had commanded troops at the front in France and had been decorated for valor".

Here the first World War is mentioned and McLendon participated in it with valor and he also got medals for his bravery in the war. From his physical appearance we get a clear picture of his character. He is bold and aggressive. He does not have the patience to listen to others and above all, he is a typical anti-black white American who indulges racism in America specially in the South America. He even does not have the patience to rely on logic. When in the barber shop, someone expresses doubts if there really happened a case of sexual abuse with Miss Minnie Cooper, he shouts:

"Happen? What the hell difference does it make? Are you going to let the black sons get away with it until one really does it?"

He intimidated the barber, Hawkshaw, when he expressed his sympathy for the black man, Will Mayes: "I know Will Mayes. It wasn't him."

McLendon whirld upon him his furious, rigid face. He told, "You mean to tell me that you'd take a nigger's word before a white woman's? Why, you damn nigger loving …". All his speeches and attitude reveal excessive hatred for that black man and all black community and in no way he wants to give them any opportunity to live peacefully. Tendency of McLendon is best described by Frued as "Death Instinct" which engenders human fancy for intoxication and in the serious and tensed moments, the temptation to escape pain by committing physical and psychological suicide. McLendon's alienation and desperation produce an contradictory effect that is a destructive attitude towards the outer world. There is no mention of McLendon's current occupation, but McLendon is entirely occupied by the fancy of his past heroism as a soldier who led his troop in the World War I. Precisely speaking, McLendon perfectly showcase the theme of dry September. His inner soul is really dry as he is abusive towards his wife at home without any proper reason. The only offend seems to him that his wife did not go to bed till he returned from outside. He not only abuse her, but also hits her physically hurting her.

McLendon became the self-declared savior of the whites in America. He angrily asks the barber, "Well, are you going to sit there and let a black son rape a white woman on the streets of Jefferson?" He is a man without heart, without conscience. When they boys dragged the Negro, Will Mayes, he felt no compassion for the helpless nigger whom they handcuffed and took to a distant place in the kiln to kill him. When Hawkshaw appealed to stop the car so that he could get out of car, McLendon did not pay heed to his requests. Rather he ordered him to jump from the running car. This is the greatest example of his heartless character. When after committing the lynching of Will Mayes, he returned home at night and saw his wife awaken, he went toward her at glanced at her with his hot eyes and sweating face. He caught her shoulder and hurt her. His wife implored, "Don't, John. I couldn't sleep… the heat; something. Please, John. You're hurting me."

However, Hawkshaw's attempts to reason with McLendon and others seems to be futile. Mayes works at an ice factory. The image of Mayes in handcuffs, unaware of his crime, is a symbol of the ongoing criminalization of black man in the post-slavery era. The pale, wan moon and its faint lights and the reference to hemorrhaging of blood, or spilling of, foreshadows the upcoming death of Will Mayes later that night.

In the screened porch, McLendon wipes the sweats due to excessive heat, undresses himself and takes his gun from his waistband and leaves it on the bedside table. Heat again even present in the story, reflecting McLendon's prejudice. He stands at the dusty screen, and pants heavily in the heat. McLendon stands on the image racial conflict in Jefferson.

(g) Charater of Will Mayes

Will Mayes may be considered as the chief protagonist of the story "Dry September", though he appears in the story only once when McLendon and his team forcefully got him in the car. He works in an ice-factory and he is accused of raping a white woman, Miss Minnie Cooper, an unmarried lady of almost 40. As a South American Nigger, Mayes draws no sympathy from the white people except Hawkshaw who repeatedly tries to advocate the mob that Will Mayes is an innocent man. But the mob has already declared him the culprit and has decided on his guilt. When on a Saturday night, while Mayes was diligently working in his ice factory, he got confused to see the angry mob. He is the representative of the black niggers who are the target of racial discrimination in South America. When the white people caught him and handcuffed him, he was confused and asked:

"What is it Captain? I ain't done nothing". But nobody listened to him. Nor they listened to the barber. They started to blow him blindly, handcuffed him, got him into the car and took him to the kiln to kill him. "Kill him, kill the son" was the instinct of the angry mob.

Faulkner craftily avoided the cruel description of lynching of Will Mayes. He rather used symbolic language that the heartless job has been done:

"Presently McLendon turned into a narrow road. It was rutted with disuse. It led back to an abandon brick kiln—a serives of reddish mounds and weed and vine-chocked vat without bottom".

In the evening of Mayer's murder, the Sanane in Jefferson was without a black fellow. No black people came there to visit the Savane. Probably they were afraid to come out; may be they were paying homage in memory of Will Mayes. Only a few white people were asking about the fate of Will Mayes. Some of them commented with a bantering tone:

"Sure. He's alright".

"All right, is he?"

"Sure. He went on a little trip."

However, will Mayes is an innocent character in the story and he attracts the sympathy not only of the barber, Hawkshaw, but of all the readers.

(h) Character of Hawkshaw

Hawkshaw, the barber, also appears in Faulkner's another story "Hair" in which he is the protagonist. ('Hair', was published in May 1931, in the *American Mercury*). The barber shop is the centre of information of the whole area of Jefferson and Hawkshaw is almost acquaintance to all. When a rumour spread about Will Mayes and Miss Minnie Cooper, Hawkshaw affirms his customers who were engaged in the gossip that Will Mayes can never commit such offence. He says:

"I know Will Mayes. He's a good nigger. And I know Miss Minnie Cooper, too". Hawkshaw is not only a information gatherer, he is a good character reader also. In response to a second barber's query, Hawkshaw said, "She's about forty, I reckon. She aint married. That's why I don't believe…". From the beginning to the end of the story Hawkshaw expressed his strong belief that Will Mayes is a good fellow and he can never commit such a heinous crime like raping an white lady. Hawkshaw is a mild-mannered white man. Rather to say, he is the conscience of lost humanity in the story. He vehemently defends Will Mayes. He is the rational fellow who is in contrast to the blind racial hatred of the other white people in his shop. He ever tries to comfort McLendon, the angry and hot-brained army officer. McLendon questions Hawkshaw's virtue as a white man. When all the white youths in his shop joins McLendon's company to punish Will Mayes, Hawkshaw also joins them with a least hope if he can keep them from killing Mayes, but he ends up jumping from the running car and limping to town in vain. Hawkshaw's amfit highlights the failure of combating racial hatred in America. Hawkshaw did not witness the killing of Mayes. He is only able to note that Mayes is not in the car on the return trip to town and he strongly takes that Mayes was murdered by them.

NOTES

NOTES

NOTES